PURSUING PUBLISHING

Pursuing Publishing
Elise By Olsen in conversation

Words by Ippolito Pestellini and Bruno Ceschel

Edited by Saúl Baeza and Elise By Olsen

ELISAVA
ISBN: 978-84-09-23684-8

Book design by Lorena G. Ortiz
Front and back cover image by Morteza Vaseghi

PURSUING PUBLISHING

Elise By Olsen in conversation

Words by Ippolito Pestellini
and Bruno Ceschel

ELISAVA

Summary

Foreword by Ippolito Pestellini 9
Conversation 13
    Introduction by Saúl Baeza 13
    Elise By Olsen in conversation with Saúl Baeza 19
Visual Resumé 45
    Selected Questions 67
Afterword by Bruno Ceschel 79

Saúl Baeza

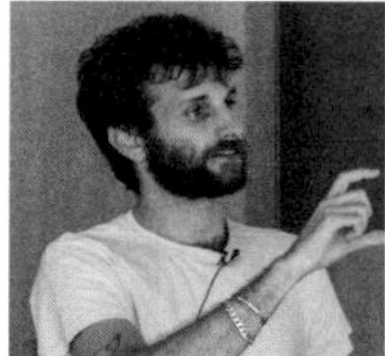
Photography by Ardila

is creative director of DOES Work, a design and consultancy practice exploring the potentials of identity in different scales and media. He is founder and editor-in-chief at VISIONS BY, a magazine focused on exploring material culture and its infinite meanings. Since 2017 he has been a curator for Understanding Design, an association whose objective is to enhance the culture of contemporary and avant-garde design in Barcelona. While lecturing at Elisavwa, he also researches functional and digital identities with the 'Future Everyday' Research Group (TU Eindhoven) and 'Futures Now' Research Group (Elisava Research).

Elise By Olsen

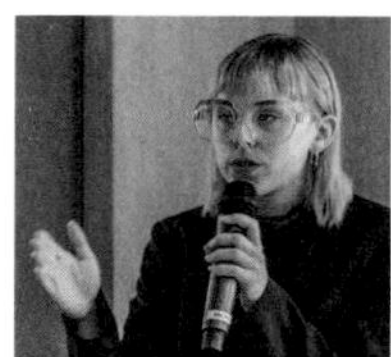
Photography by Ardila

is a Norwegian editor and publisher working within the realms of art, fashion and media. She founded youth culture magazine Recens Paper at age 13, where she held the position of editor-in-chief until her resignation in 2017. In 2018, she debuted her new fashion commentary publication Wallet, for which she now serves as editor-in-chief. With an expansive list of various projects, she has collaborated with institutions and brands such as Prada, British Fashion Council, Google Arts & Culture, Business of Fashion, TEDx, Central Saint Martins, Gucci, Facebook/ Instagram, Thaddaeus Ropac.

Bruno Ceschel

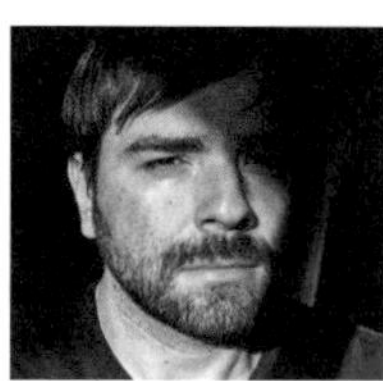
Photography by Jacques Brun

is the founder and director of Self Publish, Be Happy and a visiting lecturer at the University of the Arts London, and École Cantonale d'Art de Lausanne (ECAL). He founded Self Publish, Be Happy in 2010, and has since organized events at leading arts institutions including Tate Modern (Britain), Kunsthal Charlottenborg (Denmark), MoMA PS1 (United States) and the National Gallery of Victoria (Australia), and published books by Lucas Blalock, Carmen Winant, Lorenzo Vitturi and many more. Ceschel gives lectures and workshops internationally, and also consults for leading companies interested in contemporary photography.

Ippolito Pestellini

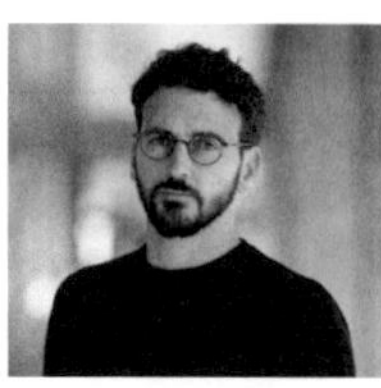
Photography by Fred Ernst

is an architect and curator based in Milan. He is the founder of the interdisciplinary agency 2050+. Through collaborations with different brands including Prada and Knoll among others, his activity extends to fashion shows, set design, product design, temporary installations, and the art direction of videos and publications. Currently he teaches at the Royal College of Arts in London. Between 2007 and 2019 he worked as an architect and partner at OMA, where his work primarily focused on research and curation, scenography and preservation.

PURSUING PUBLISHING

If there is a distinctive trait of the 21st century, it is the absence of fixed grounds: life and work unfolding through a liquid and continuous flow of experiences, trespassing disciplinary boundaries and pre-codified schemes. Creative comfort is to be found in the grey zones, in the osmotic exchange between domains and practices, in the absence of a fixed sense of belonging or boundaries. We are moving through a new landscape, one that trespasses the limits between the analogue and the digital, and most importantly one in which the definition of 'space' has become trans-scalar, trans-material, and trans-disciplinary. I was educated as an architect, but like many others I've found myself editing and curating, researching and writing, filming and event planning, staging and narrating, etc. In a sense, my practice is not so different from Elise By Olsen's.

Architecture is by all means a form of editing: it's about creating spaces and orchestrating experiences following a script, a narrative or idea. More than a discipline, it's a mind-set that allows for designing relationships, proximities, tensions and connections. That's why 'architecture' as a term is used in many contexts, for example the architecture of institutions, the architecture of an organization, the architecture of a game, the architecture of a book, the architecture of sars-cov-2 transcriptome, etc. Conversely, editing is by all means architecture as well: it is also about creating spaces – for interviews, visual essays, advertisements or pure emotions – curating their associations, and designing their relationships with a possible audience.

Elise By Olsen can be found strolling around a photo or film shoot, posing with the latest issues of her magazine, sitting down with fashion industry powerhouses for interviews, or fishing alone in the silence of a Norwegian fjord. By Olsen is the kind of person who is shaping a brand-new world. Not an editor, not a publisher, not an architect, not a curator, not a journalist, not an art-director, not a publicist, not an entrepreneur, but all of these things at once, she is a prototype of the creative professional for a new era, (finally!) marking the departure from specified forms of knowledge production.

As with some other bright examples of her generation, time is not a factor for her – or at least it doesn't proceed at the same speed as for the rest of us: at nineteen she has achieved more than others in her field have achieved in a lifetime. As a person, she is light, lucid, fast and incredibly precise, and so is her work. With the curiosity of both an explorer and an investigator, she has ventured into unknown domains, with a clear political intention: giving a voice to and facilitating space for the creativity and perspective of young people first, and tackling the mechanics and power structures of the fashion system after. In a way her work is revolutionary, a gentle uprising of young voices casting a light on their own and each other's lives, moods and creative potentials, and unveiling the conflicts and limitations of those coming before them.

By Olsen moves swiftly across territories – the latest conquest is curating contemporary art – looking for and finding the essential, intimate traits that connect us instinctively to an image, a book or an art-piece, without the need of a grand or encompassing narrative. She is the by-product of network culture, working from no fixed place with a constellation of five-hundred-plus collaborators across the world. Through absorbing and exchanging information through the fast tracks of the web, she is able to produce the most genuine and crafted analogue outputs.

('Analogue' is a word my generation has gradually lost touch with, busy as we are with embracing the latest digital frontiers, and it's both refreshing and exciting that it's gaining new traction for those younger than us.)

If publishing is an institution and a form of instituting, By Olsen is paving the way to an entire new model of cultural production, by reinventing the way to land in this brand-new world.

Several months ago, I was asked to suggest someone to deliver the closing speech at Elisava, to represent the end of the academic year. The approach was to invite someone who would link the students with their upcoming future and help them navigate this highly motivating yet anxious moment – of their reality over the last four years coming to its inexorable conclusion and the overwhelming anxiety of finding a new path in the professional world. As an Elisava alumnus myself, I remember approaching graduation day. Entering the lecture hall, looking for a spot to sit, facing the lecturer and realizing that their upcoming words were meant to mark the end of an important era. After this 60-minute lecture, some closing words and a collective applause, we were now about to be on our own.

When I was entrusted with finding the right profile for the closing speech at Elisava, I was in the middle of an email exchange with Elise By Olsen regarding her latest editorial venture. Answering one of those emails, I had a hunch, realizing that she would be the right person to invite.

I came across By Olsen's work years ago, during her editorship at Recens Paper. I had purchased some of its issues and found the idea of a bunch of super-young people expressing themselves freely and creating a vocal and visible space for their narratives encouraging. Defining culture on their own terms, with the world as their playground.
That sensation was close to what I wanted to share with

the Elisava graduating class. I thought Elise would also be able to really connect with the students, as a young person herself. She is successful - part of a system, but questioning it. Something of an authority exploring the powers involved in fashion, challenging its apparatus, pointing to the sources and speaking directly with its key actors. While accepting and understanding the ambiguity of this very present reality, blurring the boundaries of what we call disciplines and mixing them, multiplying them. Redefining the physical, the digital, and what is in between. A professional who is critical of the pre-established industry and questioning the education business. She essentially creates her own space by opening it to others.

Following some more email exchanges, scheduling issues and a week of comings and goings, it was finally settled that Elise would deliver the graduation lecture that year at Elisava. While discussing and finding the right form for her participation, we agreed on turning this traditional, and perhaps sterile, lecture format into a loose conversation, using her past, present and future projects as reference to more freely navigate through her thoughts, approaches and ideas.

A couple of weeks later, she arrived in Barcelona for the lecture and we met in person for the first time. Once in the lecture hall, we started setting up the stage: two chairs, two microphones, two bottles of water – but with an empty projector. Having not prepared any KeyNote presentation, Elise googled ‘Wallet’ and landed on a webpage showing some of the latest Wallet covers. That became the background of the conversation and the students started to enter the hall.

The following conversation took place on 27th July at 6:00 pm in the Elisava Barcelona School of Design and Engineering lecture hall, located at La Rambla, 30–32, 08002, Barcelona, Spain.

Saúl Baeza You are best known for your editorial projects such as Recens Paper and Wallet and for collaborating with big brands, institutions and corporations at a young age. We call you an editor, publisher and curator, but I'm sure that some years ago these titles weren't as clear for you as they might be today. As we will try to bridge your motivations with your results in this conversation, I think a deeper understanding of the source will help. How did it all start? Who took part? Let's start from the beginning.

Elise By Olsen Of course, I also think it's best to start from the beginning. My journey into publishing began when I was eight years old and started blogging. People sometimes laugh when I tell them this, but blogging was a very normal thing for a kid of my generation to do. In 2008, we weren't really active on social media, Instagram didn't yet exist, but blogging was something that everybody could access. You could simply create your Blogspot profile and launch your own media platform. I learned a lot about publishing from blogging – from creating a blog, basic coding, content production and marketing – actually, when I think about it, I think this is how I learned how to properly write for the first time – I learned about communicating with my audience, understanding what they wanted and then creating it, expressing what I wanted to say. This was my first encounter with media on a very, very basic level, but it was how I got interested and started: my gateway into online publishing.

My blog started out as this journal where I was posting about who I was hanging out with at school, the contents of my lunch box and what I was wearing every day, pretty much. When I was about 11 or 12, I got into Instagram and that's when a lot of magic happened. I think my generation has been very good at accessing and creating our own community online. I grew up in the suburbs of Oslo, Norway, and it didn't really have the physical community of like-minded people that I was seeking. I was with my friends at school, but I also think I wanted to choose my own friends. So online I made internet friends from all around the world and we started speaking, writing back and forth in group chats. I think this is a defining part of how we've come to be as a generation – we're open and access things that we want to access.

On group chats, I banded together with five other young Scandinavians, each with their own blogs and Instagram profiles. One of us knew a little bit of coding, I knew a little bit of writing and another did photography and video. And that was our micro editorial team. We got together and decided to create a blog network with a participating web magazine: a platform where we could all be united, that was run by and for young people only. At that time, youth-driven projects were not a thing – not just in fashion, but in the world in general – and unlike today, it was unprecedented that teenagers would have any sort of position in the global cultural conversation (outside of entertainment). But we wanted to be taken seriously, to show that we could contribute to this discussion as well, and to help define fashion and creativity on our own terms. So we made a page, called it www.archetype.nu, and it launched on May 12, 2012. On the day of the launch, the site went down due to high demand. We realized that we had struck a nerve in youth culture: we had created our own framework for young people's narratives – not just for us, but for a whole generation.

Archetype was a huge success for its premises, but meanwhile I started to go to newsstands and the magazine kiosk after school, buying magazines with my monthly allowance. At the time, a supposed 'death of print' was predicted – they were saying that paper magazines were dying. In my mind, this was a generational idea – the shock of a media generation that grew up analogue and viewed digitalization as this overpowering threat that they had to give in to. My generation grew up online and using the internet to us is as natural as walking. That has turned physical objects into a luxury: it's something we want as a contradiction to the speed, the amount of information we are exposed to online as well as networked technology. I was personally fed up with short-lived content, click-bait headlines and fast-food journalism – the 'quantity over quality' mentality that was standard for online media at the time. I missed the tangibility and tactility of print, along with the attention to detail, dedication and patience that went into it. But a lot of print publishers were not doing it right and that's why their titles were cut down on. At that point I rejected the digital in favour of the analogue, and decided to devote my time to thinking about the formula for a new contemporary print publication.

SB Having left Archetype marked the beginning of a new project. You wanted to create a print magazine by and for young people. I would say your approach was inherently ambitious, generational and global.

EBO I believed that with Archetype we had barely touched the surface of the vast network of young talent out there. I wanted to expand beyond Scandinavia and to bring a new generation of global youth's creative narratives into print and into newsstands. It was quite ambitious. However, at 13, I had absolutely no experience with print magazine production. The first issue of Recens Paper was created as a Word document, 150 pages, funded by my personal savings account (12 years of birthday money) and sent into print of a thousand copies. I didn't even know what a PDF was at that point! We obviously didn't have a designer. The issue came out with a pixelated logo, misformatted imagery and lots of grammar mistakes. It was all a mess. But the reason I'm mentioning all these mistakes – and this 'naivety' – is because I think what is really important is that we just did it. Trial and error. At first I was very sad and accepted the 'defeat', but it did for sure give me the motivation to do more, and a very solid learning curve… As well as 1000 useless copies that still remain in my dad's garage to this day.

Ahead of the second issue I started focusing on what I wanted Recens to be and on proper execution. I wanted Recens to be a good publication, regardless of it being run by young people, and that was really important to me. I also felt that there was a distinct lack of publications for young people, or the options were conventional magazines covering the topics of celebrities, beauty products and puberty, with a Disney-like approach, obviously created by adults not taking kids seriously. So for this next phase of Recens, I wanted to break with that – and to cover essential and relevant topics for youth, showcase genuine creativity – anti retouching, oppressive beauty standards and heavy advertising. I teamed up with a graphic designer/art director, a new printing house, and got proper distribution. It was very brave for a major worldwide distribution company to take us on. Recens Paper became a 200–270 page biannual title, in print only: a by-kids-for-kids operation making room for new young voices to emerge and continue to define culture on their own terms, despite the climate in which it existed. In that way it became quite ideological and activistic – a call-to-arms. Published across seven issues and featuring contributions from over 500 young people from all around the world – nearly all of them under 25 – Recens Paper finally found both an audience and a community.

SB Young people using online platforms not only to connect, but to educate themselves, to learn and to share. Discovering their needs, trying to address them. Creating their own space in order to open it for others. What was the process of creating or selecting content like?

EBO The content in Recens was a mix of commissions and submissions; we opened a submission page online where young contributors could submit their work and send photo series or poems or whatever they wanted to have featured in the magazine. It allowed young people to access our framework and our discussion. That was also a good way for us to publish very diverse content because people sent stuff from all over – obviously some shit, but a lot of really great stuff too. In a way, the whole universe around Recens Paper was online, with the end product being only in print. We were a bunch of young people sitting in each of our own bedrooms, united together through screens and group chats, creating content, communicating with our readers and doing marketing. We didn't have an office and we were all too young to travel, so there honestly wouldn't have been any Recens Paper without the internet.

SB There seems to be a very defined link between the concepts and content. Can you talk us through the themes of the various issues?

EBO I mentioned this in the TEDx talk I gave some years ago, but Recens Paper suggests a cycle through its seven themes. This reiteration draws the line of essence in coming of age. Starting from issue one, *Identify* (your personal foundations), then *Explore* (the virtual world, the physical reality, each other and ourselves), *Observe* (the sensible processes of taking notice, gathering knowledge and exchanging experience), *Invent* (your desired futures), *Share* (promoting collectivity and celebrating the spirit of teamwork) and *Document* (archiving and preserving the past, but also describing and predicting the future). Inherently this cycle can be repeated, and naturally the seventh issue was titled *Recycle* (reusing, reminiscing and referring to the past – and recycling it into a meaningful form for the contemporary).

SB Recens evolved from a Word document into a well-designed, widely distributed and internationally recognized magazine quickly. In 2016, it was listed among 'The World's Top 5 Alternative Fashion Magazines' by Highsnobiety and as part of Artforum's 'Top Magazines of 2017'. What's your approach to – and relationship with – the press?

EBO [Laughs] Let's just say early on I understood the power of the narrative and of creating myths. I have never worked with a PR agent and have always done marketing myself. Upon launching the second issue of Recens, my art director and I were discussing how we could boost the issue and get it out in international press. We figured we needed some sort of PR hook and started to write a list of options – most of them too big or costly. One day our art director called me and suggested we'd nominate me for a Guinness World Record as the 'world's youngest editor-in-chief'. I have to say that I had never thought about Guinness as something particularly spectacular – perhaps unlike my art director, who then was double my age and thought that was really cool – but decided to do it regardless. We filled out the online application form to list the record. They were going to get back to us in 12–15 weeks. Meanwhile, press started to pick up on this. I was suddenly requested for interviews on the national news in Norway, in The Guardian, Vogue, etc, with this 'youngest editor-in-chief' title. It caught the attention of Tate Modern, 10 Corso Como, Palais de Tokyo, Colette, Opening Ceremony Japan, Magma, MoMA PS1, MagCulture who all requested to stock the magazine. After some time, Guinness World Records did eventually get back to us, to inform us that they were unable to give out the title – ironically – due to their age restrictions. But it had done its job.

SB It indeed did its job of attracting the attention of bigger brands and corporations. Since the beginning, Recens Paper was financially supported by advertisers; however, your approach to ads has been quite unique.

EBO Well, there is no surprise that you need advertisers to run a print magazine financially, but I think it was important to always be clear and conscious about it, especially when you have a young readership, which brings certain responsibilities. It was important to mark our advertising as advertising and that it'd stand out from the rest of the content. In thinking about how to translate that idea visually in the magazine, my art director and I came up with a funny graphic element. We decided to add a two-centimetre 'ad warning' border around each ad. It was totally bold and transparent. So how do the advertisers feel about that? Well, first of all, we only sold the space inside of the border, so that when for example Mercedes-Benz placed an ad, they legally only owned what was inside of the border and not the whole page. And second, I would usually just say the golden line: "this is what the young people want", and get away with it. The benefit of being a young person is that you can be disruptive like this and get away with being a little bit frank. I'm sure the 'ad warning' border did grab a lot of attention to their ads regardless.

SB After six years of hard work, Recens Paper was at its peak. Then, you quit.

EBO Two years ago I was going to turn 18 and had seven issues and four years of Recens Paper behind me. As I approached 18, and was becoming an 'adult', I began to feel that my involvement in the project was becoming inauthentic and that I was at risk of exploiting youth culture in the same way so much of the industry did. What can an adult say about youth culture, when they are no longer themselves a youth? I was no longer a minor and didn't fit the role. I'd always say that running a youth magazine as an adult would be like running a student magazine as a teacher. In order to stay true to the publication's premises and mandate, I decided to step down and retire my editor-in-chief position in September 2017. For me, it was always a conscious decision: symbolic, but also personal. I wanted to get rid of this whole youth culture narrative that had framed me for years, and that was starting to be a little stigmatizing.

I also think the idea of me retiring at 17 is the perfect story to encompass the new youth-defined creative landscape where the expiration date on 'cool' looms constantly. The idea was, after all, to make space for a new generation of creative youth and to pass on the project to someone who was potentially younger than I was when I started. I announced my resignation via a documentary film, and set up an open call for a new editor to lead the magazine. Handing over the reins was a gesture of marking the importance of shifting creative voices: a lot of people with these visible or powerful positions tend to overstay. Like, for how long has Anna Wintour been at the helm of Vogue? It's really time to leave.

SB Where is Recens Paper now?

EBO Recens unfortunately remains untouched for now. We did get 200 submissions from a lot of young people who wanted to take over. But it takes time to review it all and put it back into action, because I think it's important to have the proper resources and framework accessible to an eventual successor. This also isn't something that you can push on a 13-year-old or a 16-year-old, it's something that they genuinely have to want to do. But when we pick it back up, I'm happy to give it away.

SB In the documentary you metioned before, you presented the reasons and symbolism in your decision to resign, but there is also a big intention of warning young creatives about the industry's exploitation, authority, money…

EBO I think this is an interesting dynamic worth bringing up. At the time when I was 13 and started Recens, it was unheard of that a young person would have any sort of impact within fashion and art, as I mentioned before. The industry rejected us because of our age. Now it's a whole different situation. I think the landscape responds very differently to young people now. The world today is fascinated by youth, by adolescence, by precociousness. But brands and media outlets have also realized that they depend on youth in order to fuel their corporate initiatives. As a result, young people's visions are appropriated yet not equally appreciated and capitalized on – the industry takes advantage of young people's ability to set trends, to innovate and to push limits. A usual misconception from adults working with young people is that they work for free because they 'lack experience'. Valuing and treating young people the same as adults is extremely important. Everyone's capability should be judged on the work they deliver rather than age. This scepticism to the adult dominated industries is also something that sort of fuelled my next project after Recens.

SB You embarked on a new publishing venture: Wallet. How did that come about, what was the incentive?

EBO Having one foot in, one foot out of the fashion industry for the past four years of doing Recens, there were a lot of things that I was strongly disagreeing with in the fashion industry, and a lot of powerful people I felt intimidated by. I also felt that fashion journalism had been in a poor state for a long time and that it was still far from ideal. Visual content trumped editorial; in-depth stories were branded and dependent on commercial interest and advertisers. Simultaneously, we were (and are still) being exposed to such a large amount of information and imagery every single day, and I would argue that the written word and fashion criticism is therefore increasingly important. I wanted to introduce critical thinking to ask questions, as a way of processing all this information. And I wanted to create a space for conversations that include and go beyond what we as consumers process as part of the fashion system; and ask new questions around the power, theory, politics, business and money within the fashion industry. Hence the name Wallet.

SB At that point, you already some of the themes and topics from the fashion industry that you wanted to tackle in your coming issues. Accordingly, the first issue was called 'Admins of Authority'. What was this issue about? Who are these authorities?

EBO I essentially thought 'power' seemed like a good place to start when questioning fashion, because it is a very contested term in the industry. I also have to admit that I personally also wanted to sit down with these powerful people who really intimidated me. What powers are at play? I wanted to know how those who are on top of the fashion pile regard their power. Together with my team of contributing editors, we selected three forms of power – the CEO, the buyer and the publisher – featuring Adrian Joffe, the CEO/President of Comme des Garçons and Dover Street Market, Sarah Andelman, founder and buyer of Colette and Jefferson Hack, co-founder of Dazed Media, as representatives for the respective positions. So it was the publisher, who has the power in controlling media and what you're being exposed to, and in the same way, the buyer who selects what you're going to 'get to' buy in a store, and lastly the CEO who dictates a space and a brand's direction. What kind of responsibilities do these positions entail? So I sat down with them, and of course I was also quite young, which created an interesting dynamic with these really established, very intimidating people that I tried to navigate. I remember sitting down with Sarah Andelman and asking her, "do you think the industry can survive without you?" or asking Adrian Joffe "who gains from your power as CEO, apart from from you?". They didn't expect that, they didn't expect harsh questions. I guess they thought I was going to be an innocent journalist from the school paper or something. Common to them all was that they wouldn't consider themselves as fashion authorities. Which I think is inherently a sign of power.

SB You sort of started from the beginning once again – dived straight into the source, questioning the powers, pointing out the authorities. How did you approach these powerful fashion and media moguls? How did you get the chance to sit down with them at all?

EBO For the 'Admins of Authority' issue, and for Adrian Joffe, I spent a whole year trying to get that interview locked down with him. I found his personal 'mac.com' email account, and sent him an email like, "hi, I'm Elise, I'm doing this interview about power, do you want to do it?" No reply. I had kind of given up when I actually stumbled upon him in New York and was like, "excuse me, I sent you an email to your personal email, have you seen it?" And he was like, "yeah, let's do the interview, come to Paris, 1er Place Vendôme. Let's do it." In this sense, doing a first issue about power and featuring powerful people was very strategic: it gave credibility to the publication that I was trying to create, which obviously made it a lot easier to get in touch with and talk to industry people in the next few issues. It's all about association.

SB How is Wallet structured, editorially? What can we find inside a Wallet?

EBO I believe in continuity. Each issue has a different concept and color, but the structures are the same. Wallet starts off with our Prelude, a sort of collaborative editor's letter that sets the tone of the issue, from myself and my contributing editors, then our Text Conversation, which includes long form, in-depth conversations with three different people, followed by our Visual Conversation, which is always a 20-page visual essay, a sort of re-imagined fashion editorial, if you wish, where we invite fashion practitioners to interpret the issue's theme, and finished off with our Postlude, a short after-thought or reflection of the issue. At the very end we have a notes spread, for you to take notes in – and take notes from – and these can also be ripped out. I usually try to do the interviews myself, directly and, as long as it's possible, face to face.

SB The power issue marked the beginning of a wider critical interest in the fashion industry and system. What other topics followed in the coming issues?

EBO So we did the power issue, 'Admins of Authority', where in addition to the three interviews I mentioned, the Visual Conversation asked 20 fashion workers, of any sort, that are affected by power to use their craft to explore what such powers symbolize to them visually. Then the 'Pioneers of Publishing' issue, which was a conversation on the evolution of fashion press and the mechanisms within it. What is fashion publishing today? We did conversations with fashion publishers, of micro-press and of publishing conglomerates, to understand where 'the magazine' sits in today's complex media landscape, physically and digitally. The issue featured Isabella Burley, Editor-in-Chief of Dazed & Confused, Nick Knight, Director of SHOWstudio and Joerg Koch, Editor-in-Chief of 032c and SSENSE and questioned whether they maintain, challenge or ignore the frames and formats of traditional publishing. For the issue's Visual Conversation, we asked for contributions as facsimiles – the traditional technique of reproducing books and prints as true to the original source as possible. We invited 20 fashion practitioners we admire, who also use publishing as a medium, to contribute facsimiles of their own publications – including lookbooks, catalogues, magazines and so on. We then did 'Elite of Education', which was a conversation on fashion academia and its changing operations. How is fashion studied, taught and theorized today? We spoke to three educators, who in one way or another are responsible for educating the fashion workers of the future. Hussein Chalayan, professor of fashion at the University of Applied Arts Vienna, took part, along with Hywel Davies, fashion programme director at Central Saint Martins and Shelley Fox who is the Donna Karan professor of fashion at Parsons School of Design. The Visual Conversation was a prospectus of the emerging players of the fashion industry of tomorrow, wherein we invited students and recent graduates from a wide array of global fashion schools to present their portfolios freely.

Then we have also done space volume one: the 'Shamans of Space' issue, which was about discursive and creative spaces of fashion, from designers' studios to fashion's traditional mode of presentation – the runway and fashion exhibitions; all the different physical rooms, but also metaphysical rooms. I sat down with fashion designer Grace Wales Bonner, fashion curator Matthew Linde as well as architect and partner of OMA/AMO Ippolito Laparelli to have an expanded conversation around where fashion happens. For the Visual Conversation we created a 20-page visual essay contextualizing all the various modes of fashion space. Volume Two was the 'Champions of Commerce' issue, our fifth and most recent issue as of today. We looked into commercial space and the marketplaces of fashion. How can clothing in a store behave today? Through interviews with Rami Atallah, CEO of SSENSE, Vittorio Radice, director of La Rinascente as well as Arun Gupta, CEO of Grailed, we questioned the enduring appeal and importance of physical space, the symbiotic relationship between commerce and creativity and how the digital user experience has shaped the way we shop. The visual conversation featured imagery of various commercial fashion spaces, both current and archival – ranging from luxury brand stores, independent boutiques, high street chain stores, shopping malls, online 'Big Cartel' stores and 'alternative' shops.

[Exhales] I could have talked about all of these issues for ages.

SB From what I understand, you always wanted Wallet to be a printed magazine only: a physical object. How did you translate that intention into the design and format?

EBO The format started as a conceptual spin-off on the name: we called the publication Wallet because of its premise in speaking to the major financial clout of an increasingly global industry. There has also been a trend of doing all these big and weighty coffee table books and magazines, which are not convenient. Wallet, by comparison, is pocket-sized. The format aimed to compliment the concept of an actual wallet, for it to be easy to keep with you – portable, mobile and accessible – and for it to function as one of your essentials. In the wake of this predicted death of print, we had to rethink the way we do print for a younger generation. Our research question was: "What if you could have a physical publication in a mobile format that you can carry around with your essentials?" We wanted to adapt it to the accessibility and behaviour of the iPhone, too, so you are actually able to carry Wallet with you and it's compact with information. So the magazine is pocket-sized, suiting a standard jeans pocket (11 by 22 centimetres). Design-wise it's a tricky format because it's so small, so how do you maximize the space you have? In a way, Wallet is very anti 'coffee table'...

SB Wallet too was funded by advertising. And once again, you decided to approach them similarly to how you did with Recens Paper. Inside Wallet the ads are perforated, so the readers can rip them out!

EBO Yes and I'm always trying to push this dynamic between the advertiser and the reader. I guess I believe that you cannot really be exploited if you exploit back. So another critical element in Wallet is our approach to ads. Most magazines rely on advertising to run, and we do feature ads, but those in Wallet can be ripped out if you'd rather read the issue without them. They have a perforation down the side so they can be torn out cleanly. You can tear out the ads and throw them away, or you can hang them up on your wall – whatever you like. In fashion magazines there's typically a lot of ads, and sometimes it gets very distracting from the content. And then you can wonder how Gucci, Prada and Chanel, our major advertisers, react to this. Similarly to Recens, we told them not to have any sensitive information in the first centimetres on the side of their ads and that "this is what the young people want"... But I actually do believe that the reader, whether young or old, appreciates our transparency about the ads and that we mark them very clearly as advertising. I think it also encourages the reader to actively interact with their Wallet.

SB This reminds me of how you can block out the ads on digital platforms such as YouTube or Google.

EBO Yeah, it's sort of like an analogue version of AdBlock. That's what we call it, the analogue AdBlock.

SB Why was it so important for you to address the state of fashion criticism? What's the role of a fashion critic today?

EBO I generally think it's a huge misconception that fashion criticism is limited to collection reviews or reports on celebrities' sartorial choices. Yes, it's an important form of expression, but I think institutional critique in fashion is increasingly important, because it has huge economic power in the world. Plus the fashion system in general is very complex structurally, and there's a lot to grapple with. I hope that criticism in fashion will be just as respected as criticism in other cultural endeavours such as art, film or music. But I think the problem is that fashion isn't necessarily taken seriously in the first place, I think partly because it's looked upon as a 'feminine' and 'fun' field, and partly due to fashion's close relationship with commerce. So much of the text in fashion, or fashion journalism, is funded by the fashion houses and brands, so consequently it *will* be hard to to have critical integrity. I mean, these magazines' and writers' entire economies and lifestyles are fully dependent on receiving product sponsorships, attending dinner events or being flown in and accommodated at fashion shows! I think the key to critical journalism, versus fashion coverage, is having an outsider's perspective and a certain distance. Free and independent press, the written word and analytical writing will always be important, maybe especially in fashion, so there needs to be more organization and more external funding for the critics doing it. We now see critical debates initiated with the new generation, which has happened very publicly and very powerfully. I hope and think fashion criticism will have a resurgence soon.

SB You have used your project to expose necessary debates. If you are correct and fashion criticism will have a resurgence, what's the future of Wallet? Is the fashion system a limitless resource for criticism?

EBO I believe in conversations and see Wallet as a series of holistic discussions – each issue speaking with another, in a way. We invite the reader to actively partake in the conversation, while our internal process is based on having dynamic discussions around everything that we publish. I treat each issue of Wallet as its own separate publication, each with its own specific theme, though the frames and format we work with remain the same. In that sense I believe in continuity. In total we will do 10 issues of Wallet about the fashion industry, and then the box set will be completed. I think that's what makes sense and we have been operating with that timeframe in mind. Eventually the plan is to apply some of these broad themes to other industries and do 10 new issues of Wallet about the art market, music industry, food, etc. As long as there's money present, I think there's a lot to be questioned in all sorts of industries.

SB It's quite surprising that you are not scared of starting a project and then directing its end – either in advance or throughout the process. This isn't common practice within the publishing industry. I think it requires a lot of effort to have such a valid approach. You basically build everything up: a team, define an editorial structure, bring advertisers in, get money, plan distribution, and so on, just to dissect or destroy it all once it's done. Or at least, detach yourself from it. It happened with Recens and now you're saying it will happen to Wallet.

EBO Yes, I have a very specific duration to all of my projects. I have always had this specific narrative in mind. Recens was a very social and ideological kind of project, while Wallet is a more mature, text-based project, and then maybe after this, I would want to go and do a highly commercial magazine or a visual publication or fashion image-making. Or no publishing at all.

SB Besides your role as an editor and publisher, you curate exhibitions. Is that a discipline you approach in the same way as you do with your editing or publishing? Has it been an organic evolution?

EBO In a lot of ways, I think editing a magazine and curating go very much hand in hand. What I essentially have been doing through my publishing is curating – whether it's selecting what talent to feature, narrating a photo series or combining different notions together into a holistic package or issue. Facilitating. In that sense, the only difference is the medium – whether you use the physical room or the printed page – but the process is more or less the same. It wasn't like I was making strategic moves towards trying to be a curator, it was more that I was invited to do a residency in 2017: the annual 89plus programme at Google Arts & Culture in Paris. 89plus is not a curatorial residency, so I believe I was the first non-artist participating, but it was definitely an interesting opportunity to explore the use of technology in my curatorial and publishing practice. When arriving, I understood that I wanted to examine the very essence of Google: the democratization of information, in the form of an exhibition. I wanted to make this exhibition globally available and that could happen online by creating a new access point. Together with one of the Google Arts & Culture's software engineers, I started building a digital space that could extend on the experience of the physical space. Just like how an event that is captured and shared on Instagram lives on forever, I wanted to challenge the duration of an exhibition and to see if an exhibition could not only be documented, but actually live on – and potentially develop – on the internet. 'Early Works' was a one-night exhibition honouring the early works in the early stages of 10 global and emerging artists, who create intuitively across mediums. The access point featured a 360-degree animated online documentation of the show, and was accompanied by a YouTube interview series with each of the artists. After completing the residency and doing this exhibition, I started continuously listing and cataloguing emerging artists and their early works. I think 'Early Works' has the potential of growing into an ongoing project, becoming a series of exhibitions, a book, or whatever form it might take. But again, publishing and curating might be institutionally and economically quite different, but perhaps methodologically much the same.

SB In your work, there is always a dichotomy I find really interesting; you always propose a dialogue between the physical and the digital. On one hand, for your editorial projects, you have been using digital platforms and the internet to connect and generate new content, although publishing it physically. On the other hand, this returns in your curatorial practice, and once you had the chance to curate an exhibition for a big gallery you decided to approach it digitally. Is this a constant exercise for you?

EBO A few months after this residency I was approached by Julia Peyton-Jones, who is the director of Thaddaeus Ropac, a major London gallery. She was organizing a solo show of paintings by fellow Norwegian and artist Bjarne Melgaard, and wanted me to programme some sort of digital part for a younger audience. Rather than a digital commission purely documenting the exhibition online, I suggested treating the show as a duplex: semi-digital and semi-physical, meaning that the gallery exhibition would be displayed in tandem with a virtual extension. The idea was that Bjarne was going to select younger artists from our hometown Oslo, that he was influenced by in one way or the other, to be involved in the exhibition. We uploaded their work on Ropac's Instagram page dynamically, 50 posts over the course of – and in parallel with – the gallery exhibition. It was fun to collaborate with this very luxurious, established bluechip gallery that has been around for a long time, and use their platform to completely disrupt and break with what they usually do.

I think it's interesting that everybody's trying – whether gallery or museum directors, artists or even publishers – to distinguish heavily between digital and physical media. Almost treating them like two competing formats that you have to choose between. I think there's magic in merging the two – maximizing the digital format and maximizing the physical format. What can the physical offer that the digital cannot, and vice versa? Even with Wallet's Instagram, which is the only online platform we use, we're trying to not simply *digitize* the printed content, but to *expand* on the conversation and create an *extension* of the content. Now Wallet is fairly cheap, only eight euros, which was a conscious decision from our side, but print magazines are at the end of the day unaccessible for many. The internet, on the other hand, is way more democratic.

I do admit that digital publishing has been a contested term for me, but it's clear that there's a real appetite for online publications, and that digital media offers a lot of things for both the publisher and the reader. Instant access to a wide range of content, direct and dynamic interaction with an audience and endless technological possibilities. At the end of the day, online publishing sits differently in the media landscape now – artistically, symbolically and even economically – compared to my time at Archetype for example. There's a new pace, new programming, new demands, a new rhyme and a new reason. When it comes to it, I'm not opposed to internet publishing, but it for sure has to be done right. And for this Ropac project, it was exciting to amalgamate my interests in both media and art.

SB You've been appointed Chief Curator for a major Norwegian touring exhibition in 2020. What can we expect?

EBO Yes, I was asked by this monumental Norwegian exhibition called Vestlandsutstillingen – it's sort of like a biennale format – to curate their 2020 edition. It's a touring exhibition that's travelling to six different museums and 'kunsthalls' in Norway. It's been around since 1922. I think it was daring of them to ask me since I don't have an art education or a crazy portfolio of exhibitions, but it's also interesting to give my take on their very established framework – and premises of showcasing artists holding a connection to Western Norway specifically. What does it even mean to have a connection to someplace today? We're living in a time where participating in artistic discourse outside of one's local existence is possible. As a response, the 2020 edition of Vestlandsutstillingen will explore the quintessential 'Norwegian' in relation to the quintessential 'international' in contemporary art. The Norwegian west coastal landscape is inherently vibrant, with a very heavy association to the era of national romanticism, which is visible to the area's artists at all times and thus inevitable. For this exhibition I'm thinking about how the landscape and its history sculpts art to this day. In the wake of a digital revolution, which is free from the mental and physical boundaries of time and space, is it possible to rethink and recontextualize national romanticism today? I've selected artists who still engage in close dialogue with their surroundings – through, for example, organic processes, time-consuming methods and solid materials. The 2020 edition rejects expectations of curatorial unity and geographical affiliation in favour of spontaneous, and surprisingly analogue, tensions between materials, works and the audience.

SB Before this conversation today, we were talking with Albert Fuster, the academic director of Elisava, about the pros and cons of design education and education in general – the system, its structure, and its expected results. But you don't have a university degree yourself. How do you then validate the content you consume?

EBO Well, I didn't even finish high school. It wasn't that I didn't enjoy school, because I did, and I still think it's a very important time that gives you time to discipline and reflect, but I simply didn't have time. During my first half year in high school my career started to accelerate like never before. I was offered new projects, opportunities and more travelling, which essentially raised the (risky) question of whether to stay in school or to give in to my work. I was enrolled in a media high school, but I had already been practising in the media industry for many years. I also felt really critical of these teachers trying to be authoritarian figures, and that I had access to knowledge and a huge network online that I wanted to explore on my own. So that really did it for me. One day I just stopped showing up to class. Ever since, I've been very focused on constantly trying to teach myself through reading books, going to conferences and, perhaps most importantly, having good conversations with a lot of different people. In many ways, every issue of Wallet is also some sort of thesis, where I'm learning so much about every aspect of the fashion and media industry, and beyond. And, perhaps paradoxically, I've started to do occasional lectures at various universities: at Oslo School of Architecture and Design, Bocconi in Milan, Central Saint Martins in London, LaSalle College in Montreal, Parsons New York, Polimoda in Florence and here in Barcelona at Elisava. I'm not yet used to it – you have to understand that most of these students are older than myself which creates a weird dynamic – and I don't necessarily feel comfortable with traditional teaching either. Who am I to educate someone else? What I can do is to have conversations with students and teach by doing. I think it's a good test for now. And also, I have to say that I've been very lucky to have very supportive parents that let me make my own choices, whether it's regarding school or otherwise, and even if they don't have a clue about what I really do for a living.

SB Do you read magazines yourself?

EBO Yeah, of course I do. I'm a publisher, so I'm obviously immersed in fashion publishing at large and feel a responsibility to stay updated on the field. And I've been a collector of books, magazines and other publications for the longest time. So I still drop by the newsstand very often and still get clavicle pain from lugging around backpacks full of them when travelling. I was recently lecturing at Central Saint Martins when one of the students asked me to recommend a reading list for fashion research, and I couldn't think of a single publication. Obviously I could recommend a lot of fabulous visual fashion magazines, but publications for research... I ended up sending the student home with a reading list totally unrelated to fashion. I guess this leads back to it not being a tradition or discipline for fashion research, journalism, criticism – brain food. I still love good magazines dedicated to fashion image making, but also magazines and printed matter about art, culture, music, comics, literature, etc.

SB Who is the Wallet reader or consumer?

EBO I think demographics are quite irrelevant to be honest, I used to read the newspaper when I was five and can read children's books now. But our readership is a mix between young people that sort of matured with me from the Recens era, and industry people. We're not trying to make fashion such an exclusive and narrow space, Wallet is for anybody who's interested in criticism in a new form, whether from art or from fashion or from architecture. Surprisingly, a lot of architects actually read Wallet; I don't know why that is, if it's the logo or whatever that's appealing to them. On that note, there's an interesting conversation with Françoise Mouly [publisher of comics magazine Raw and art editor of The New Yorker] in the latest issue of Apartamento, where she speaks about the idea of 'editing as architecture', which I really liked. I also think publishing, by all means, is a form of architecture. What we essentially do as publishers and editors is to make space, frameworks, structures – and build sites for ourselves and others to occupy and work within. Like the architects, we conceive physical and material objects, albeit on different terms – whether as a building or as a book. We curate connections – whether visual, linguistic, social, material, symbolic, intellectual, emotional. The process of printing a book and its mechanisms – choosing its paper, form and size, finishing and details, to the actual execution and printing – is essentially building through printing.

SB Apropos this idea of editing as architecture, you have been working closely with art director Morteza Vaseghi for a long time. How does that dynamic work?

EBO Yes, I've worked alongside Morteza on all my projects; both Recens and Wallet, and beyond. Last year we also established Ecudorp, which is an executive media group and our joint venture. We do projects within consulting, creative direction and content production, in addition to publishing catalogues, books and our own titles. That is a very strong and valuable collaboration. He is the visual counterpart to all these ideas, translating content into design and concept. Morteza is double my age, so it's an interesting dynamic, a sort of counter-generational handshake that has proven to be very successful. We have a lot of fun too, in always thinking about how to make advertisers angry or disrupt publishing or fashion. He has taught me to always have a holistic, and provisional, approach in everything I do.

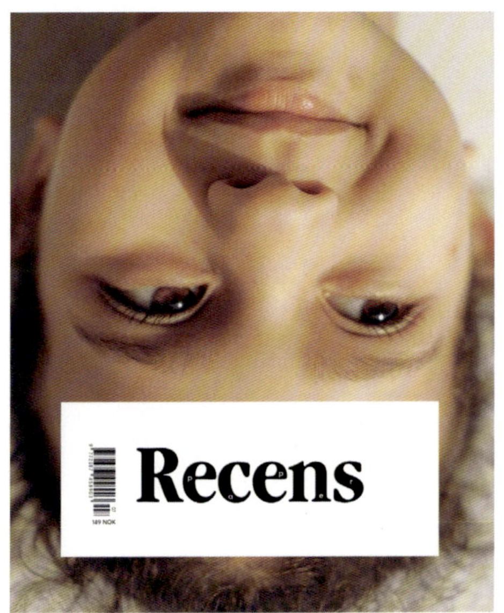
Recens
149 NOK

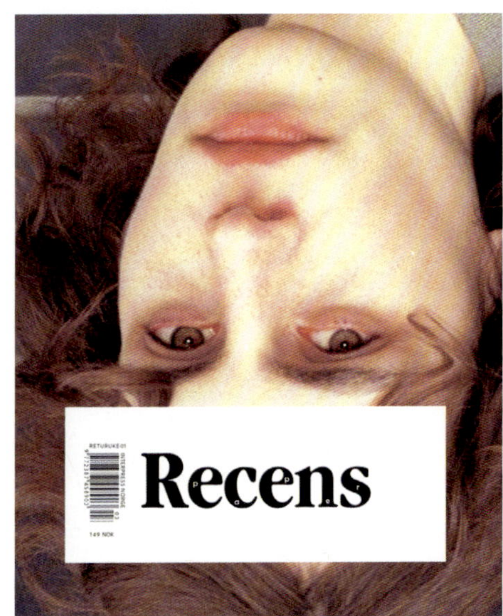
Recens
149 NOK

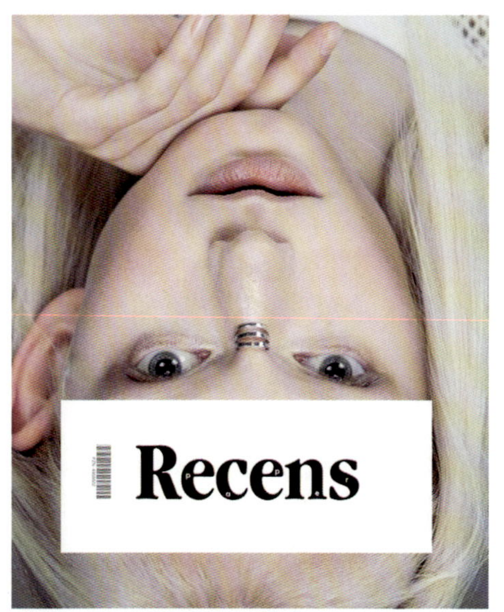
Recens

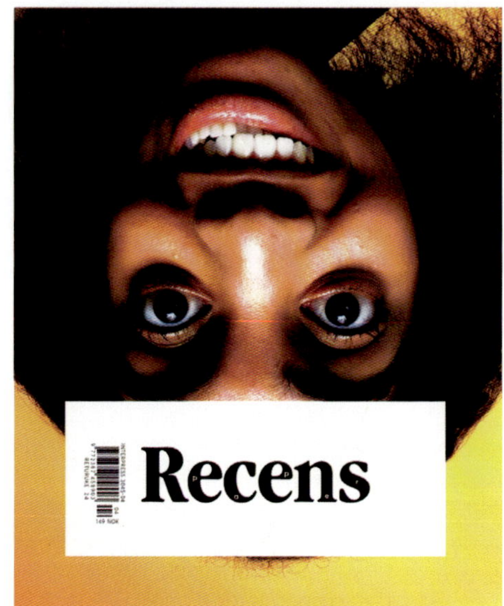
Recens
149 NOK

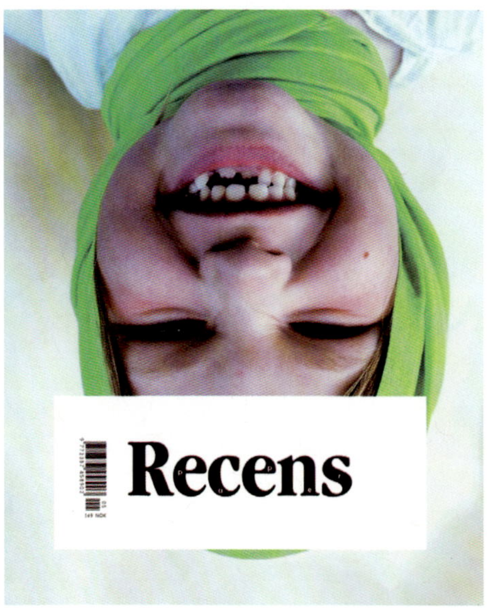
Recens
149 NOK

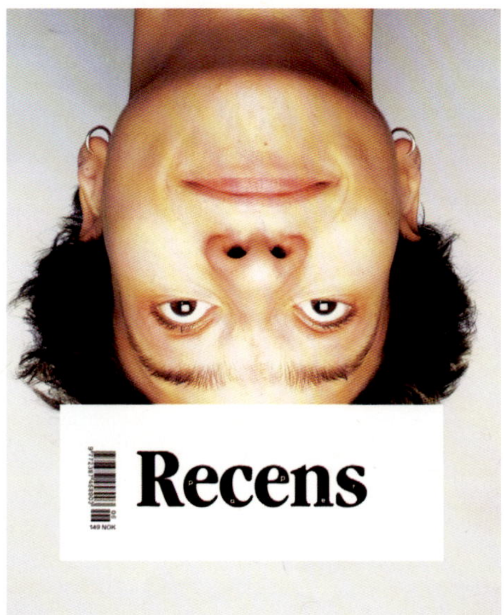
Recens
149 NOK

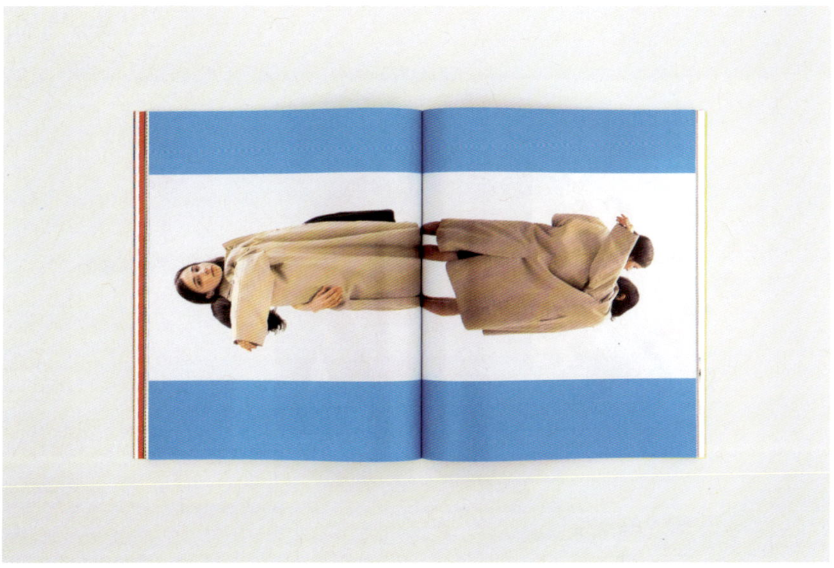

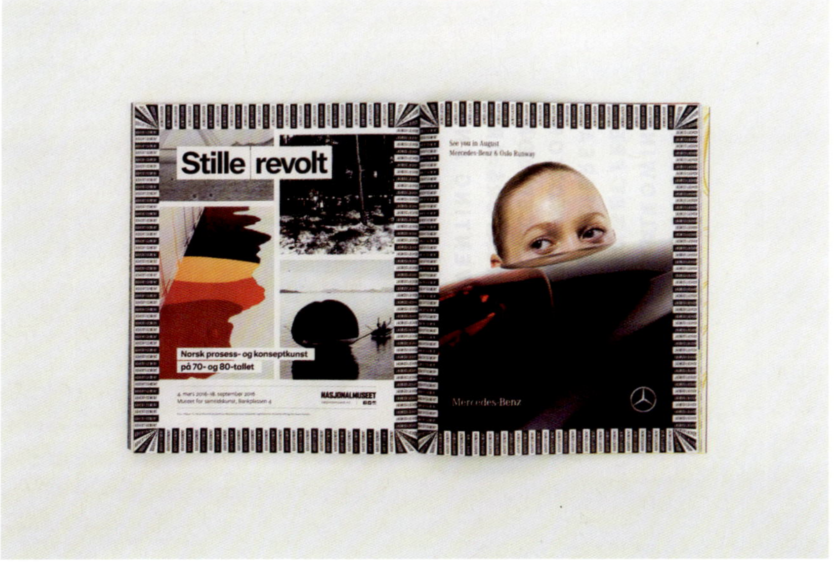
Stille revolt
Norsk prosess- og konseptkunst
på 70- og 80-tallet
4. mars 2016–18. september 2016
Museet for samtidskunst, Bankplassen 4
NASJONALMUSEET
See you in August
Mercedes-Benz & Oslo Runway
Mercedes-Benz

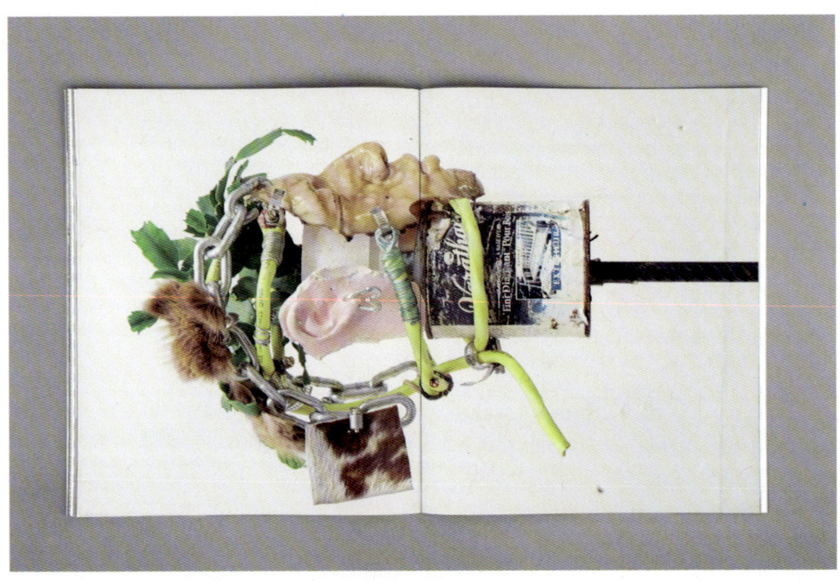

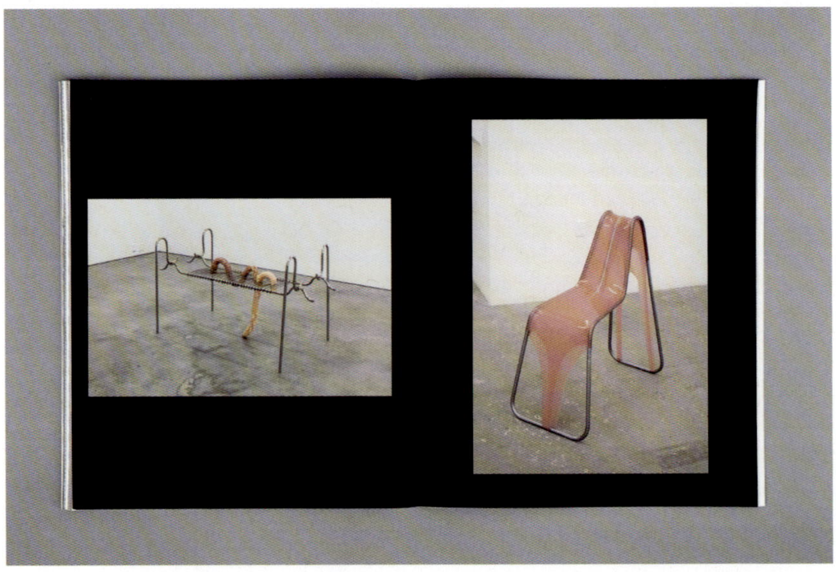

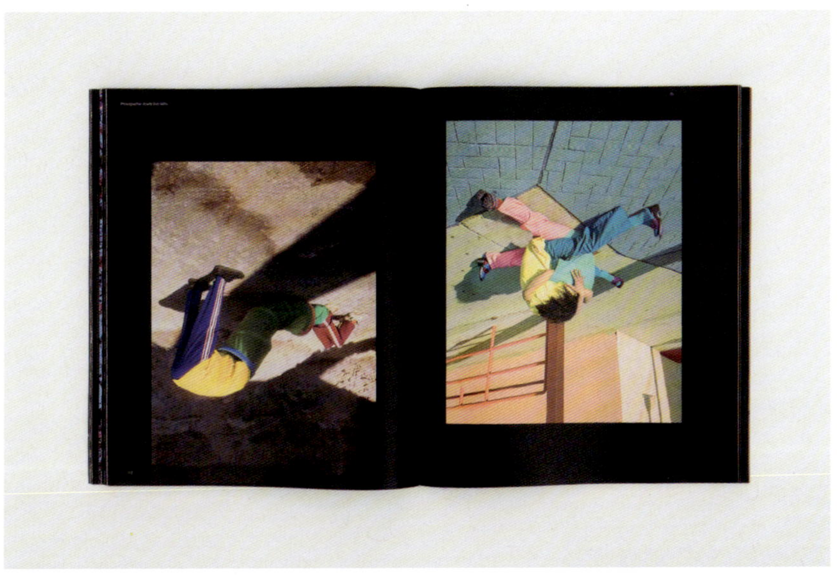

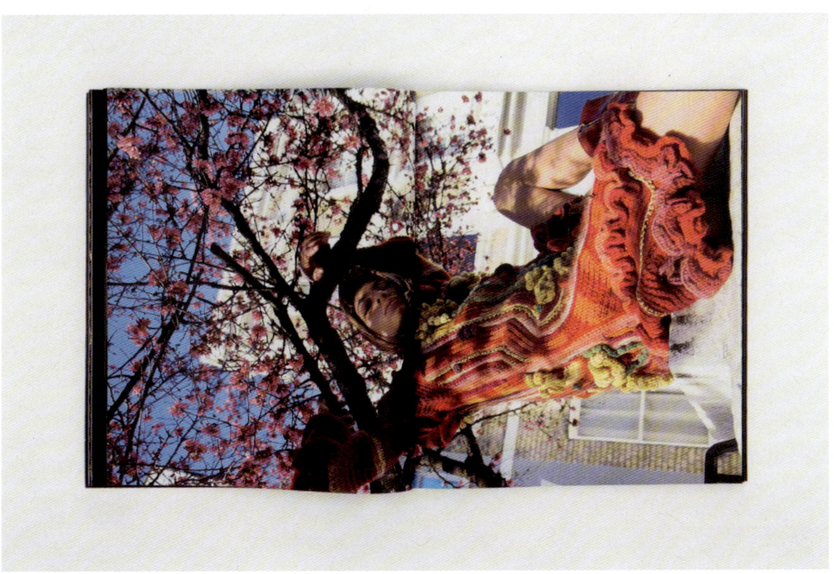

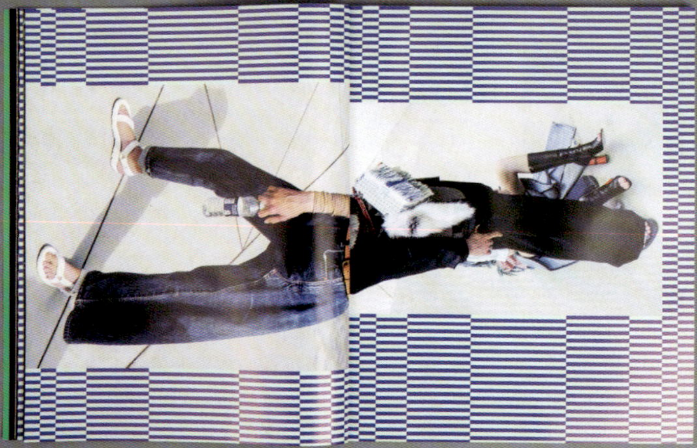

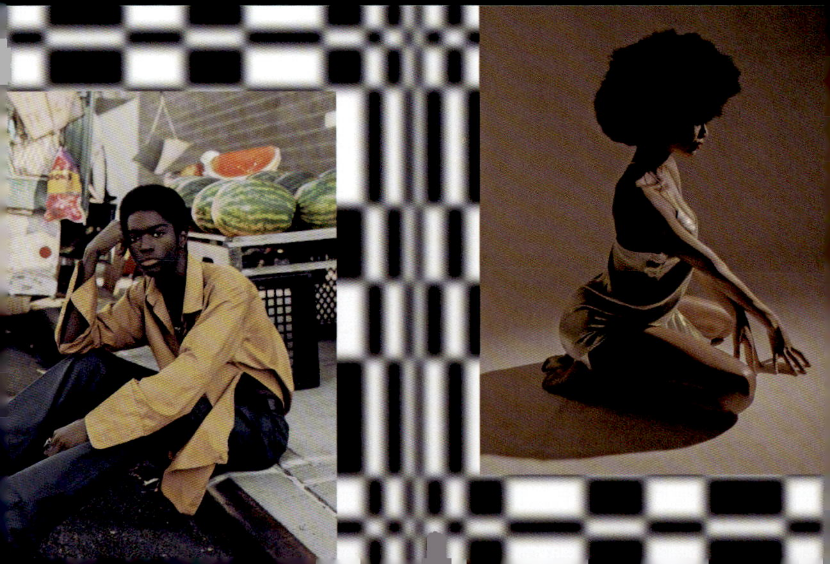

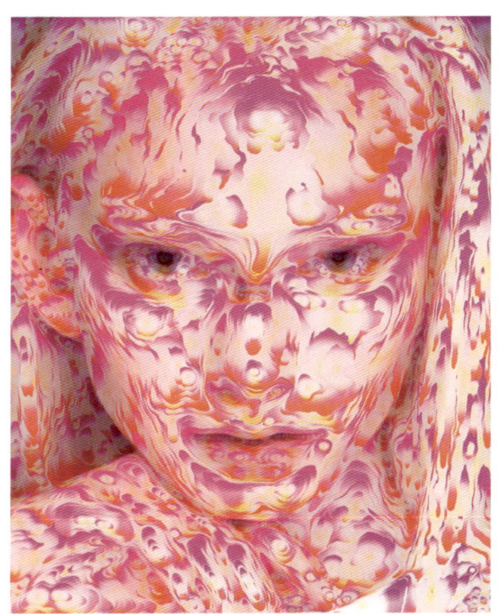

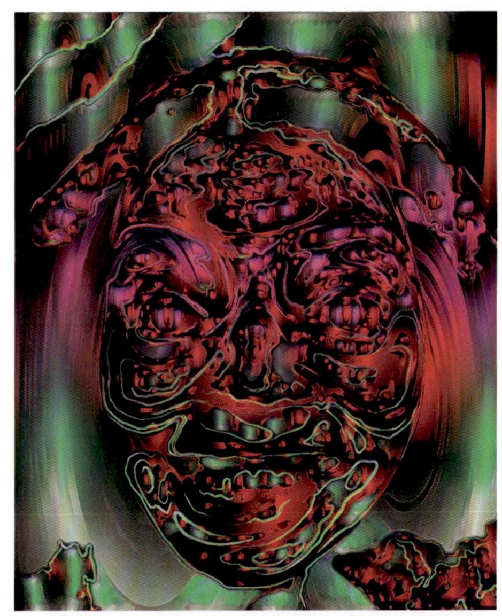

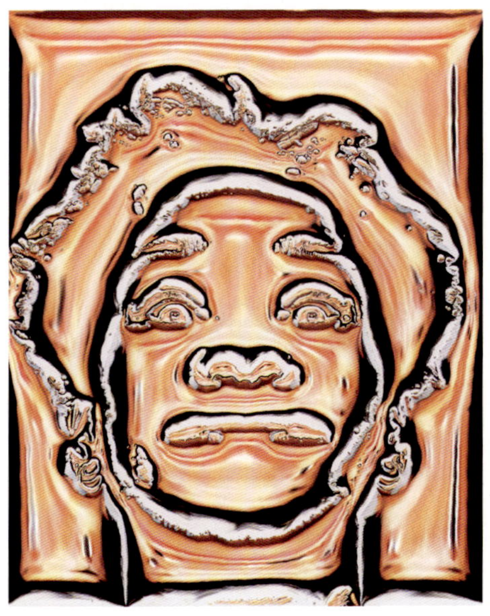

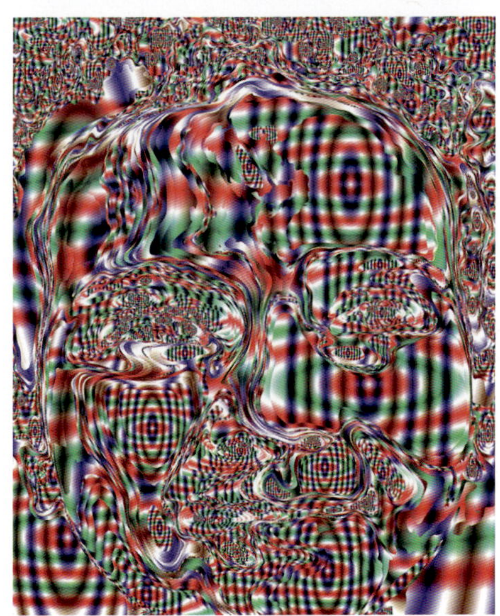

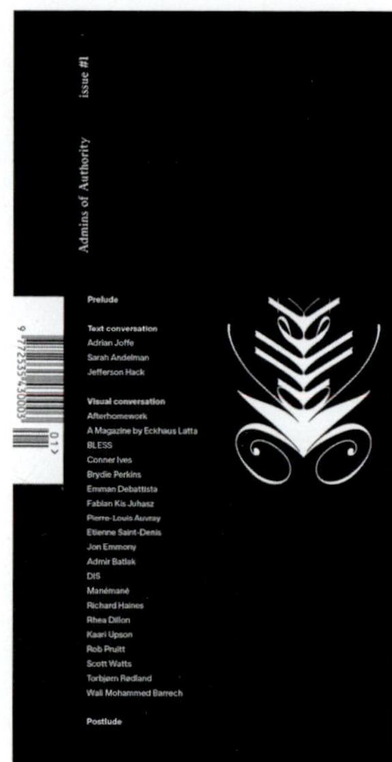
Admins of Authority
issue #1
Prelude
Text conversation
Adrian Joffe
Sarah Andelman
Jefferson Hack
Visual conversation
Afterhomework
A Magazine by Eckhaus Latta
BLESS
Conner Ives
Brydie Perkins
Emman Debattista
Fabian Kis Juhasz
Pierre-Louis Auvray
Etienne Saint-Denis
Jon Emmony
Admir Batlak
DIS
Manémané
Richard Haines
Rhea Dillon
Kaari Upson
Rob Pruitt
Scott Watts
Torbjørn Rødland
Wali Mohammed Barrech
Postlude

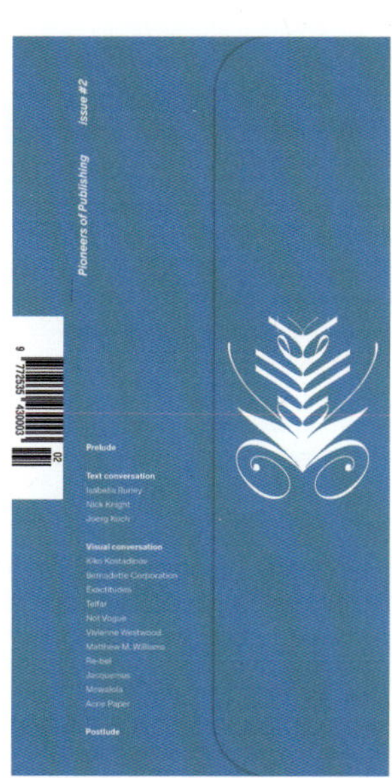
Pioneers of Publishing
issue #2
Prelude
Text conversation
Isabella Burley
Nick Knight
Joerg Koch
Visual conversation
Kiko Kostadinov
Bernadette Corporation
Exactitudes
Telfar
Not Vogue
Vivienne Westwood
Matthew M. Williams
Re-bel
Jacquemus
Mowalola
Acne Paper
Postlude

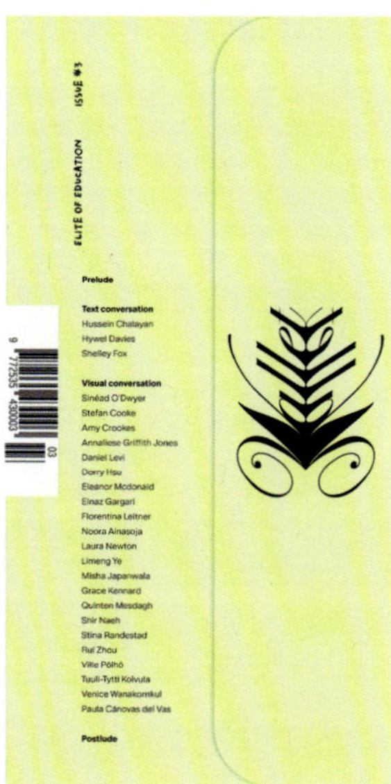
ELITE OF EDUCATION
ISSUE #3
Prelude
Text conversation
Hussein Chalayan
Hywel Davies
Shelley Fox
Visual conversation
Sinéad O'Dwyer
Stefan Cooke
Amy Crookes
Annaliese Griffith Jones
Daniel Levi
Dorry Hsu
Eleanor Mcdonald
Elnaz Gargari
Florentina Leitner
Noora Ainasoja
Laura Newton
Limeng Ye
Misha Japanwala
Grace Kennard
Quinten Mesdagh
Shir Naeh
Stina Randestad
Rui Zhou
Ville Pölhö
Tuuli-Tytti Koivula
Venice Wanakornkul
Paula Cánovas del Vas
Postlude

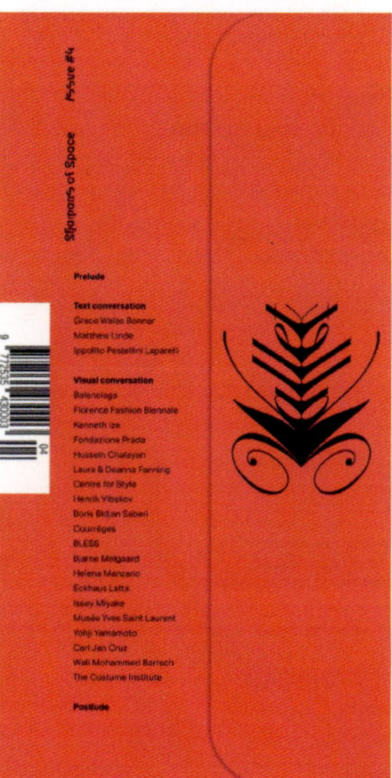
Shamans of Space
Issue #4
Prelude
Text conversation
Grace Wales Bonner
Matthew Linde
Ippolito Pestellini Laparelli
Visual conversation
Balenciaga
Florence Fashion Biennale
Kenneth Ize
Fondazione Prada
Hussein Chalayan
Laura & Deanna Fanning
Centre for Style
Henrik Vibskov
Boris Bidjan Saberi
Courrèges
BLESS
Bjarne Melgaard
Helena Manzano
Eckhaus Latta
Issey Miyake
Musée Yves Saint Laurent
Yohji Yamamoto
Carl Jan Cruz
Wali Mohammed Barrech
The Costume Institute
Postlude

9 772535 430003 05
Prelude
Text conversation
Visual conversation
H&M
Stand Up Comedy
Dover Street Market
Gallery 909
Ooga Booga
Colette
The House of Beauty and Culture
Camper
Balenciaga
LN-CC
The Broken Arm
Barneys
Slam Jam
Postlude

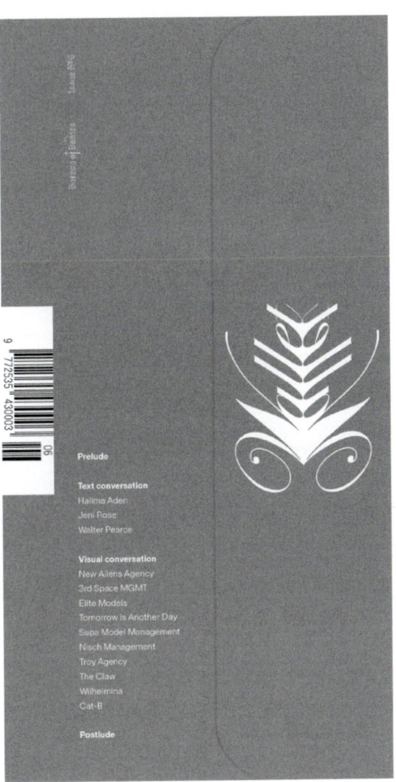
9 772535 430003 06
Prelude
Text conversation
Halima Aden
Jeni Rose
Walter Pearce
Visual conversation
New Aliens Agency
3rd Space MGMT
Elite Models
Tomorrow Is Another Day
Supa Model Management
Nisch Management
Troy Agency
The Claw
Wilhelmina
Cat-B
Postlude

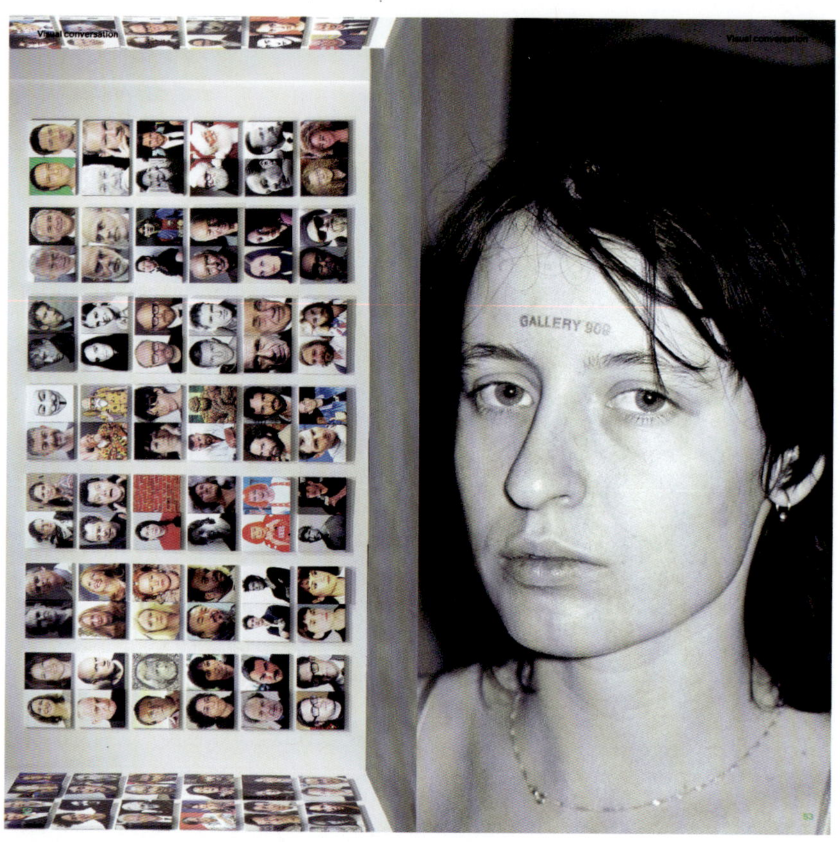
Visual conversation
Visual conversation
GALLERY 909

Sinead O'Dwyer (Royal College of Art London, MA Womenswear)

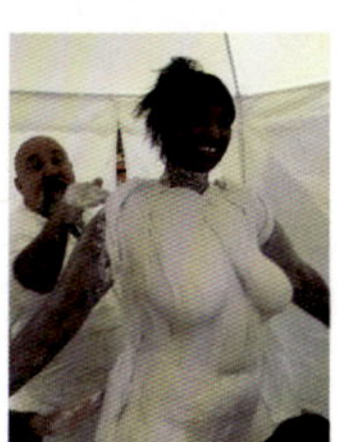

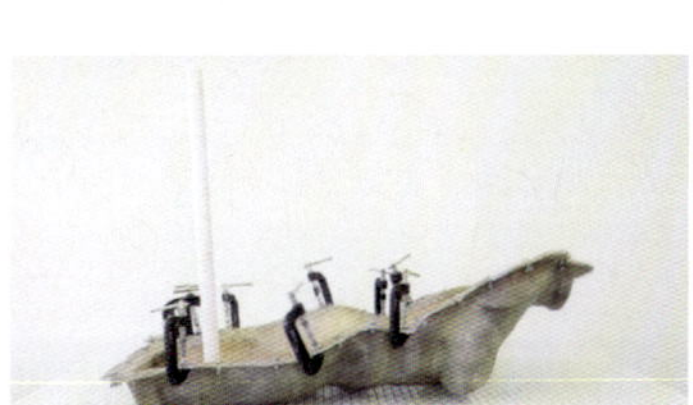

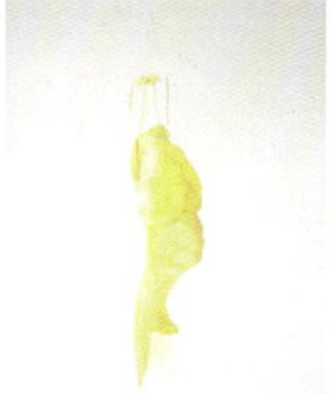

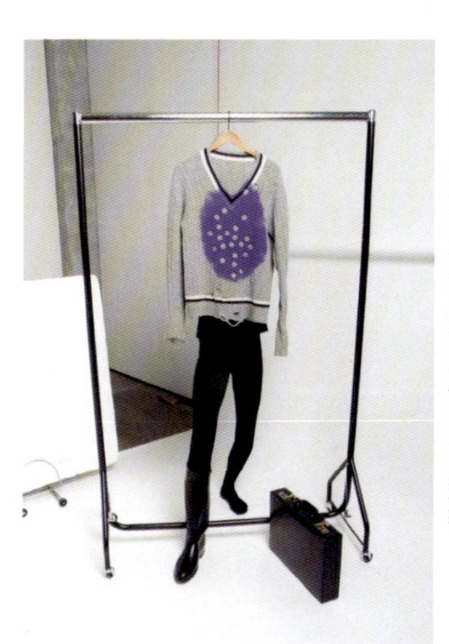

Stefan Cooke (Central Saint Martins, MA Fashion Textiles)

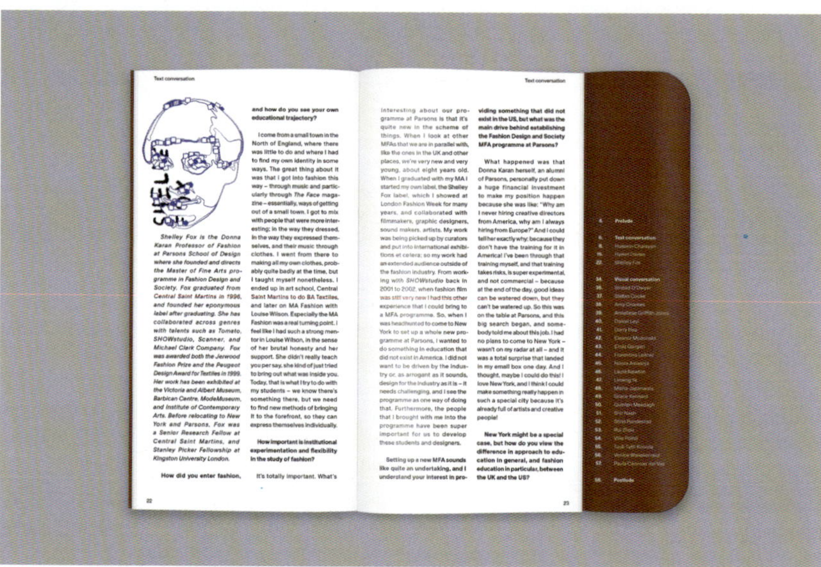

Text conversation

Shelley Fox is the Donna Karan Professor of Fashion at Parsons School of Design where she founded and directs the Master of Fine Arts programme in Fashion Design and Society. Fox graduated from Central Saint Martins in 1996, and founded her eponymous label after graduating. She has collaborated across genres with talents such as Tomato, SHOWstudio, Scanner, and Michael Clark Company. Fox was awarded both the Jerwood Fashion Prize and the Peugeot Design Award for Textiles in 1999. Her work has been exhibited at the Victoria and Albert Museum, Barbican Centre, ModeMuseum, and Institute of Contemporary Arts. Before relocating to New York and Parsons, Fox was a Senior Research Fellow at Central Saint Martins, and Stanley Picker Fellowship at Kingston University London.

How did you enter fashion, and how do you see your own educational trajectory?

I come from a small town in the North of England, where there was little to do and where I had to find my own identity in some ways. The great thing about it was that I got into fashion this way – through music and particularly through *The Face* magazine – essentially, ways of getting out of a small town. I got to mix with people that were more interesting; in the way they dressed, in the way they expressed themselves, and their music through clothes. I went from there to making all my own clothes, probably quite badly at the time, but I taught myself nonetheless. I ended up in art school, Central Saint Martins to do BA Textiles, and later on MA Fashion with Louise Wilson. Especially the MA Fashion was a real turning point. I feel like I had such a strong mentor in Louise Wilson, in the sense of her brutal honesty and her support. She didn't really teach you per say, she kind of just tried to bring out what was inside you. Today, that is what I try to do with my students – we know there's something there, but we need to find new methods of bringing it to the forefront, so they can express themselves individually.

How important is institutional experimentation and flexibility in the study of fashion?

It's totally important. What's interesting about our programme at Parsons is that it's quite new in the scheme of things. When I look at other MFAs that we are in parallel with, like the ones in the UK and other places, we're very new and very young, about eight years old. When I graduated with my MA I started my own label, the Shelley Fox label, which I showed at London Fashion Week for many years, and collaborated with filmmakers, graphic designers, sound makers, artists. My work was being picked up by curators and put into international exhibitions et cetera; so my work had an extended audience outside of the fashion industry. From working with *SHOWstudio* back in 2001 to 2002, when fashion film was still very new I had this other experience that I could bring to a MFA programme. So, when I was headhunted to come to New York to set up a whole new programme at Parsons, I wanted to do something in education that did not exist in America. I did not want to be driven by the industry or, as arrogant as it sounds, design for the industry as it is – it needs challenging, and I see the programme as one way of doing that. Furthermore, the people that I brought with me into the programme have been super important for us to develop these students and designers.

Setting up a new MFA sounds like quite an undertaking, and I understand your interest in providing something that did not exist in the US, but what was the main drive behind establishing the Fashion Design and Society MFA programme at Parsons?

What happened was that Donna Karan herself, an alumni of Parsons, personally put down a huge financial investment to make my position happen because she was like: "Why am I never hiring creative directors from America, why am I always hiring from Europe?" And I could tell her exactly why: because they don't have the training for it in America! I've been through that training myself, and that training takes risks, is super experimental, and not commercial – because at the end of the day, good ideas can be watered down, but they can't be watered up. So this was on the table at Parsons, and this big search began, and somebody told me about this job. I had no plans to come to New York – wasn't on my radar at all – and it was a total surprise that landed in my email box one day. And I thought, maybe I could do this! I love New York, and I think I could make something really happen in such a special city because it's already full of artists and creative people!

New York might be a special case, but how do you view the difference in approach to education in general, and fashion education in particular, between the UK and the US?

22 23

4. Prelude
6. Text conversation
8. [illegible]
15. [illegible]
22. Shelley Fox
34. Visual conversation
36.–57. [illegible]
58. Postlude

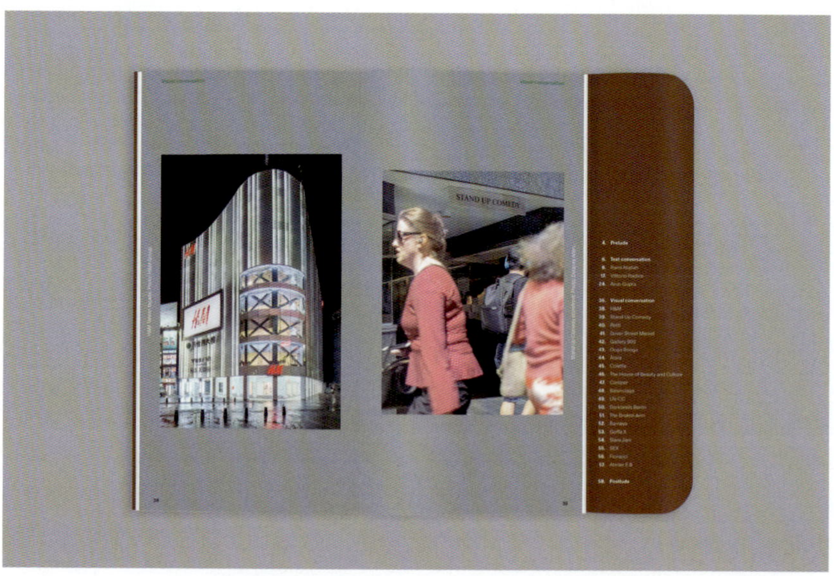

4. Prelude
6. Text conversation
8. [illegible]
17. [illegible]
24. [illegible]
36. Visual conversation
38. H&M
39. Stand Up Comedy
40. [illegible]
41. Dover Street Market
42.–45. [illegible]
46. The House of Beauty and Culture
47. Camper
48.–50. [illegible]
51. The Broken Arm
52.–54. [illegible]
55. SEX
56.–57. [illegible]
58. Postlude

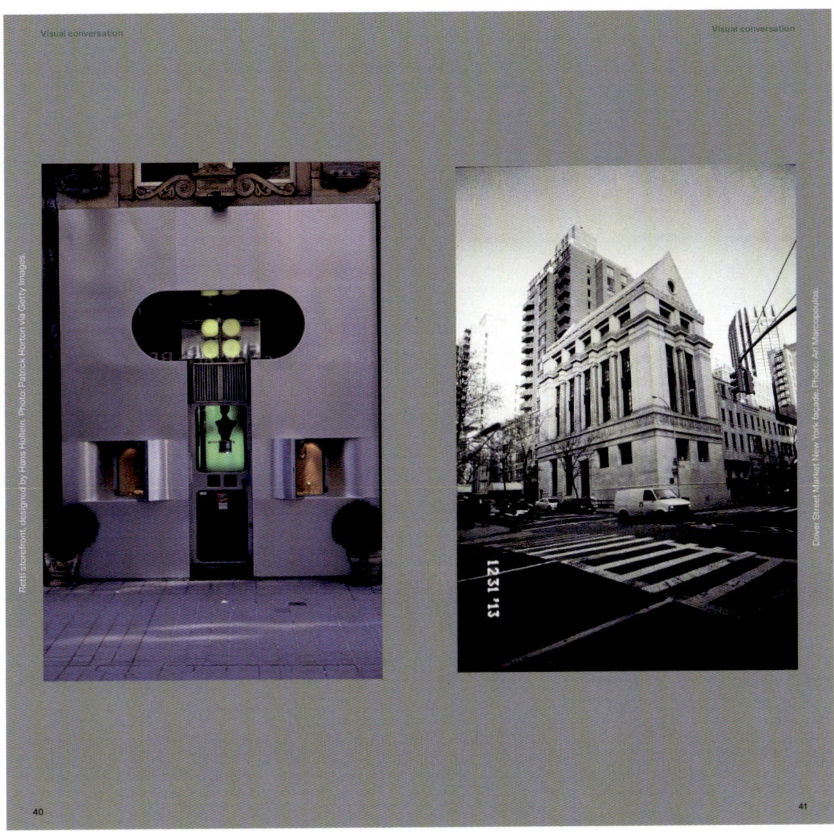
Visual conversation
Retti storefront, designed by Hans Hollein. Photo: Patrick Horton via Getty Images.
40
Visual conversation
1231 '13
Dover Street Market New York façade. Photo: Ari Marcopoulos.
41

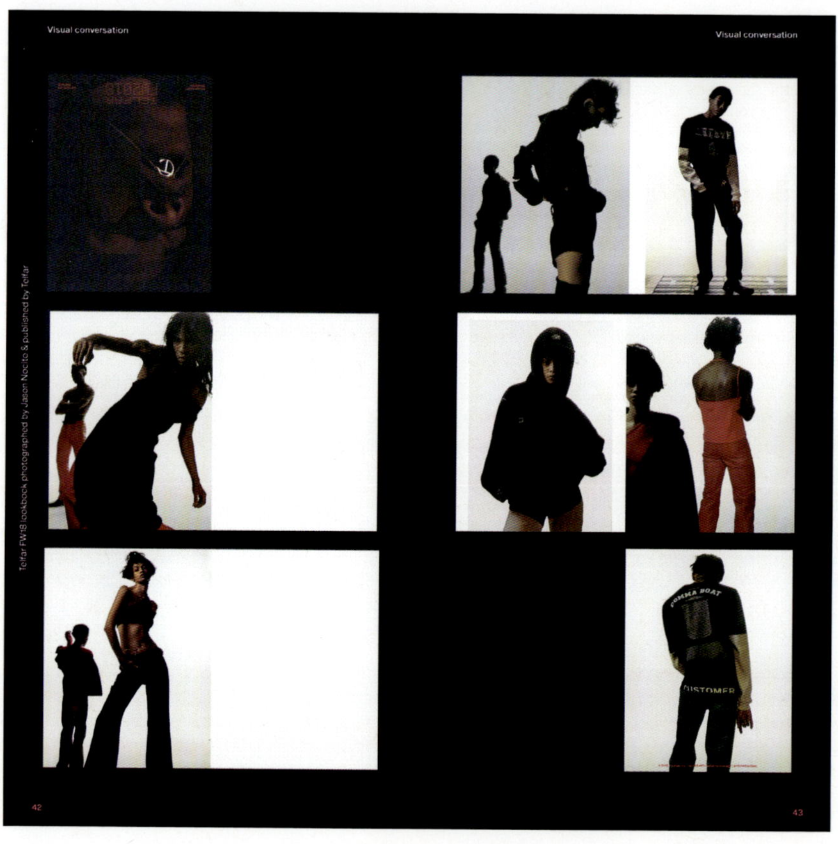
Visual conversation
Visual conversation
Telfar FW18 lookbook photographed by Jason Nocito & published by Telfar
42
43

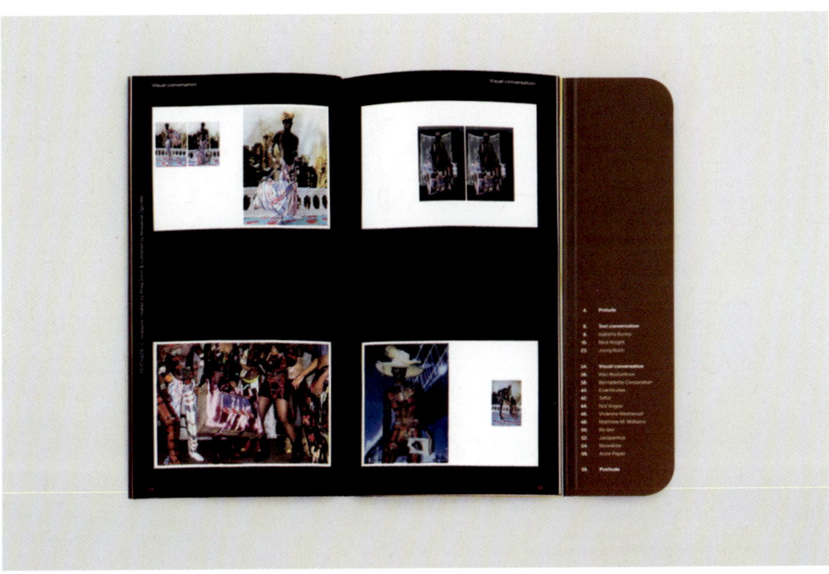

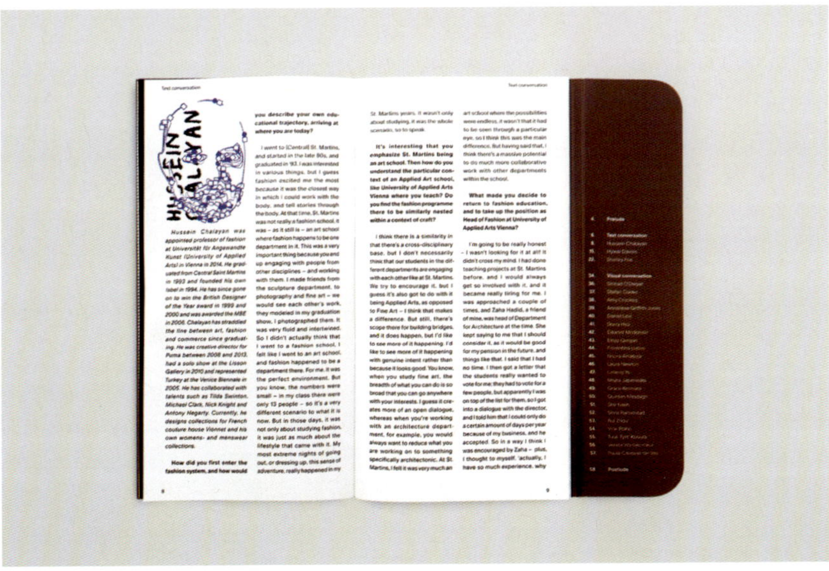

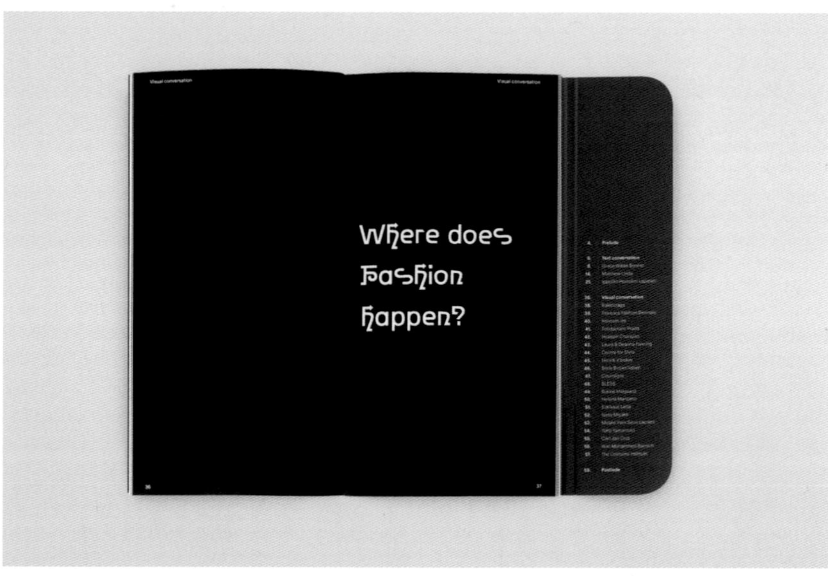
Where does
Fashion
happen?

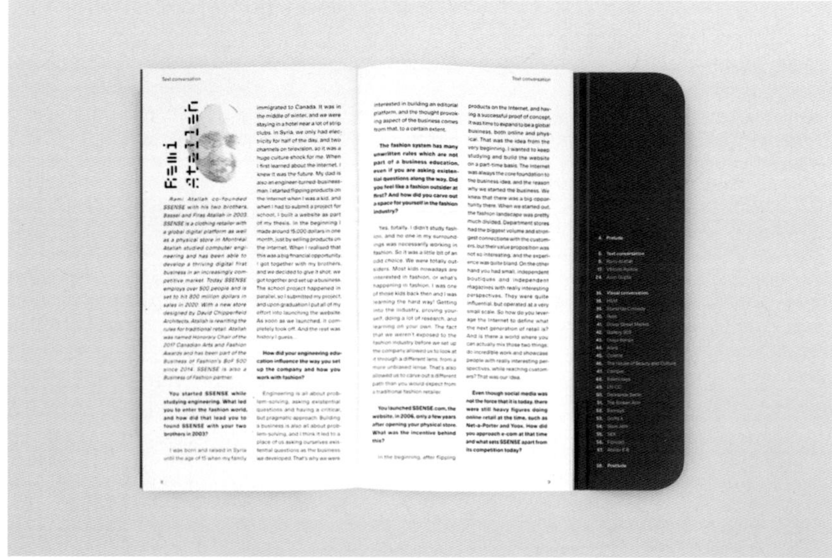

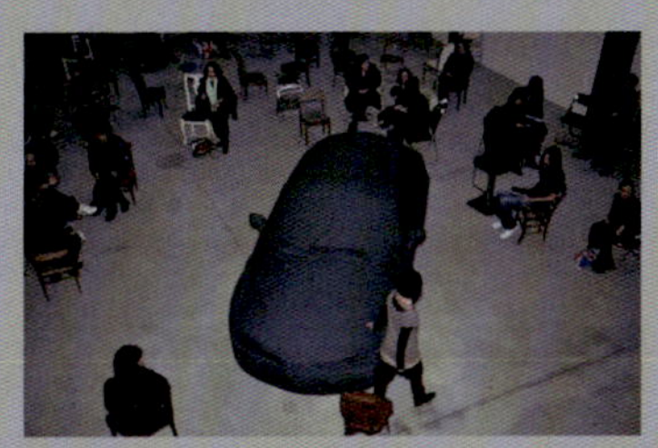

BLESS N°34 "Eperfct Verything" fashion presentation. Courtesy of BLESS.

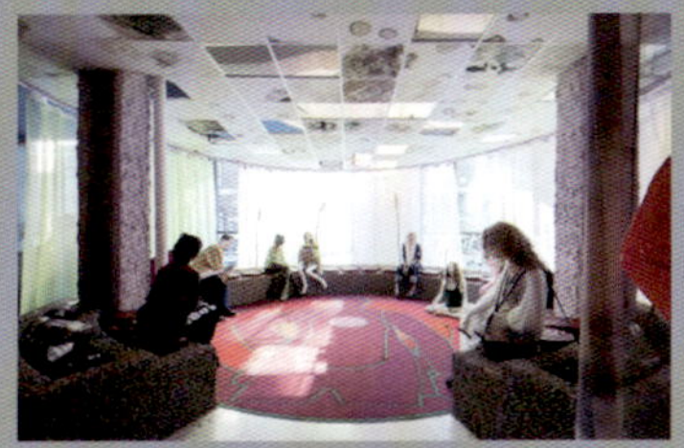

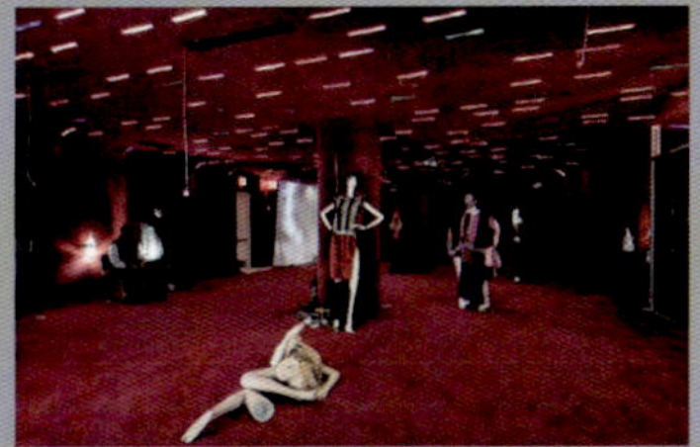

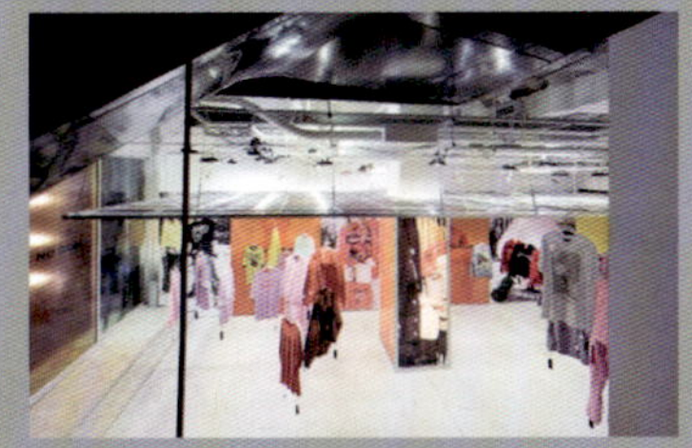

Bjarne Melgaard "The Casual Pleasure of Disappointment" exhibition at Red Bull Arts. Courtesy of Gavin Brown.

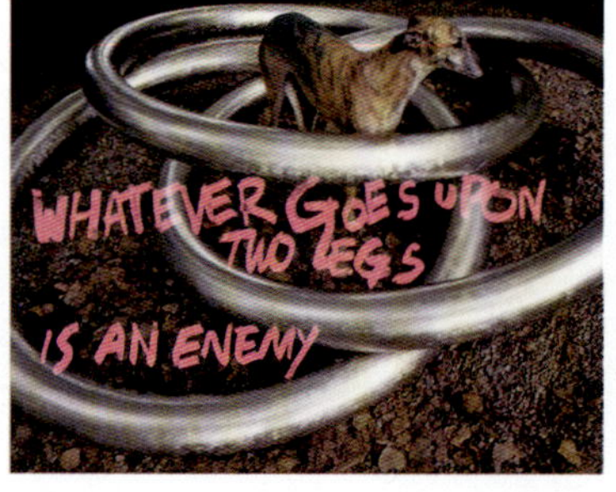
WHATEVER GOES UPON
TWO LEGS
IS AN ENEMY

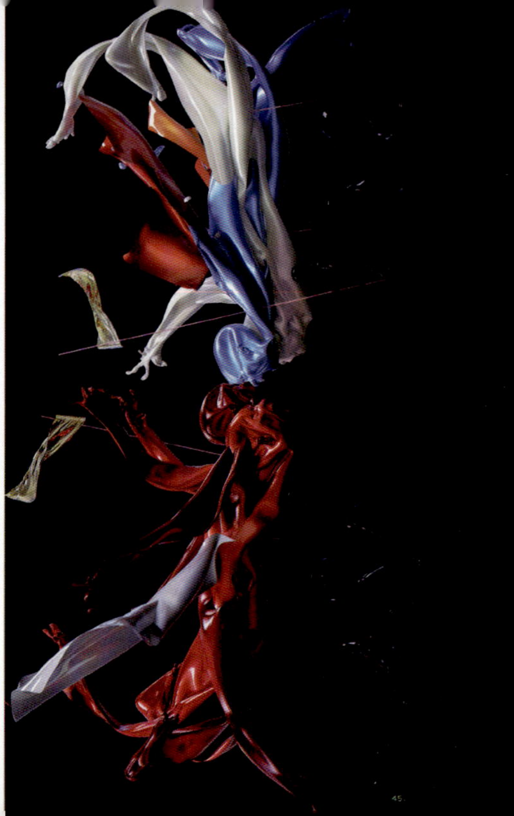

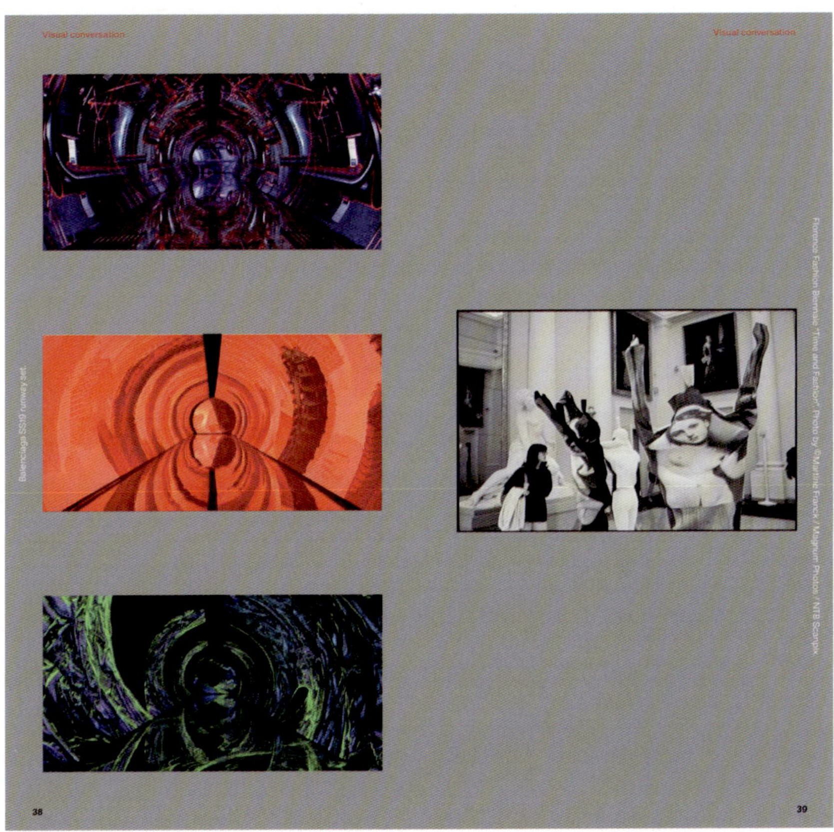
Visual conversation
Visual conversation
Balenciaga SS19 runway set.
Florence Fashion Biennale "Time and Fashion". Photo by ©Martine Franck / Magnum Photos / NTB Scanpix
38
39

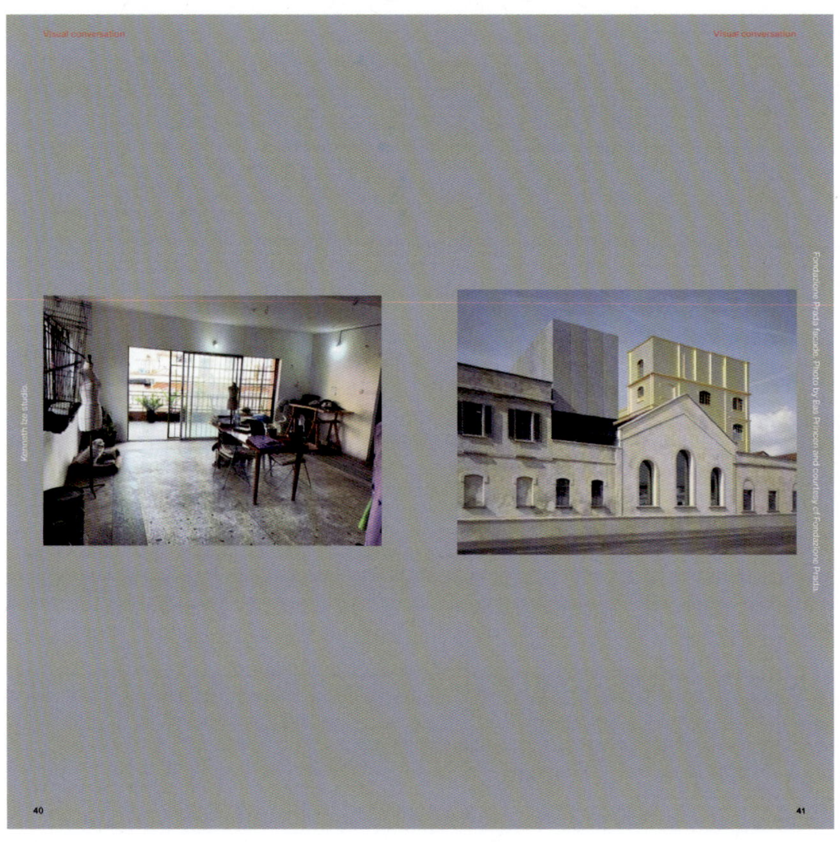
Visual conversation
Visual conversation
Kenneth Ize studio.
Fondazione Prada facade. Photo by Bas Princen and courtesy of Fondazione Prada.
40
41

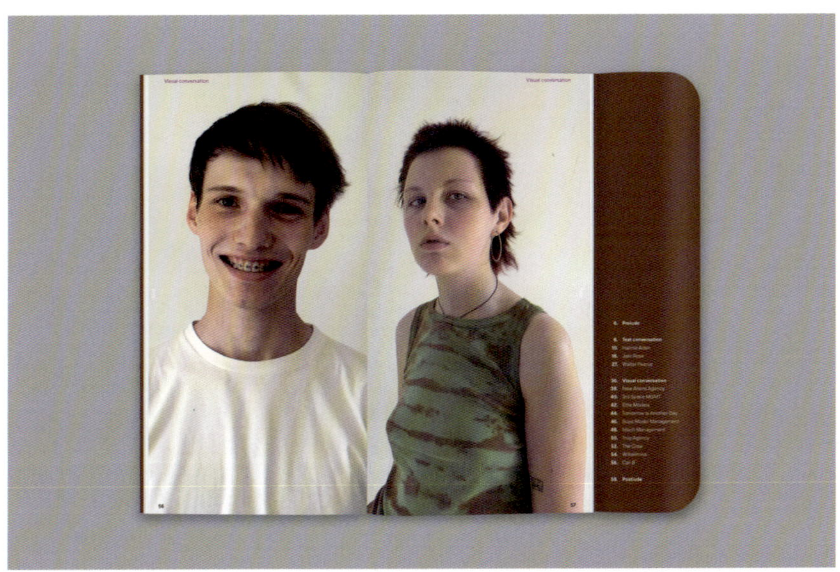

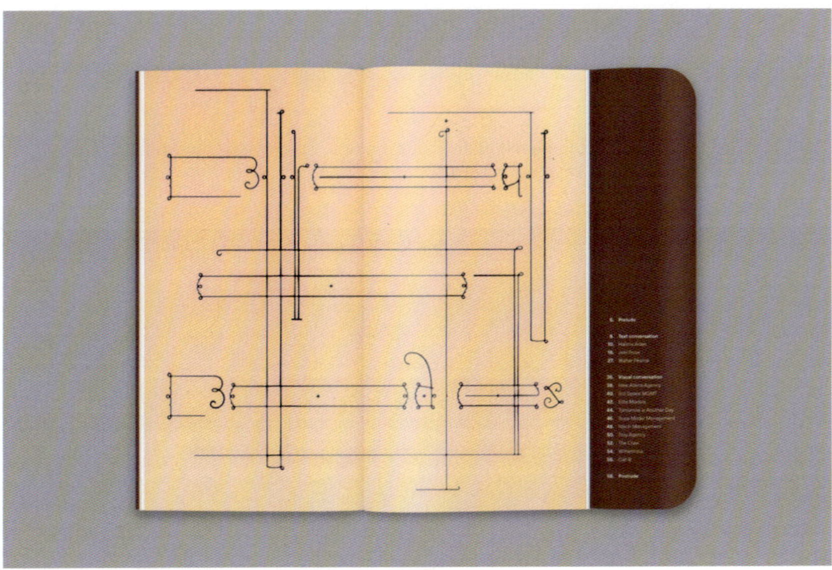

Saúl Baeza
Let's open up for questions from the audience!

Elise By Osen
It's always more interesting to hear what the audience would actually be curious to hear about, rather than me just going on talking. I'll be around after too, so we can also do a one-to-one.

Audience member
It feels like you have a strong character, I mean it's admirable really. Do you think it was maybe your personality or was it more that it's a product of the world you've gone through, the editing world, the fashion and all that. Have you become more rough by it?

EBO
That's up to you to judge, but thank you so much! That's so nice to hear. I'm not sure if it was a product of the industry, but perhaps more a reaction to the industry. I think, when you're really young and you're working in any adult-dominated industry, they don't usually want to hear you out. They don't want you to stand up and speak. I'm a shy person – maybe not now, but I used to be – so I really had to toughen up. There's been so many times where there have been issues and challenges with advertisers not paying me, with printing houses or some-

one asking me to consult for them and paying ridiculously little money and stuff like that. You just have to stand up for yourself. And by me standing up for myself, I stand up for all the other young people, it's a collective effort.

AM

It's really inspiring that as such a young person you're standing up for yourself. And as you said, you are also standing up for every other young person out there.

EBO

Thank you. Thank you.

AM

Being that young, how did you get that voice or that name in this big adult-dominated industry? As you said, is it just being rude and stubborn?

EBO

Am I just now teaching you how to be rude and stubborn? Of course we have to be polite and listen to your parents. [Laughs] Jokes aside, I think the internet gave me access to a vast network in the first place, in the beginning. But I also think that nowadays, stuff is not so complicated. If you want to speak to Obama, you can basically DM him on Instagram. It's not like it used to be. You can basically speak to anybody you want or reach out to people, so if you want to start a fashion brand, you can make an Instagram account and be half way there. This is how I did it, but it's not just me. It's a whole generation, this is the way we do things now and I think we're extremely lucky and very privileged to be able to have this 'forum' on the internet. I think we should milk that.

SB
Any other questions?

AM
Hi, I have two questions, they're a little bit different. First, what is the logo about? It looks very interesting. It looks like a fish bone, how did you create that? Secondly, what do young people stand for now, what is interesting for them in fashion, in design, in general?

EBO
First things first. About the logo. A lot of people hate this logo. I hear it a lot: "Oh my God, what an ugly logo!" I think it's funny, perhaps it's just ahead of its time. It will grow on them. It basically says 'Wallet' in this very bridal-like font, and then it's mirrored symmetrically. When Morteza created it, I think it was a very love-hate approach. He wanted some sort of reaction, whether good or bad. It was intriguing. When we started Wallet, the design industry or the design notion at the time was very minimal and perfect and sans serif and 90s futuristic or whatever. Everything looked the same. So he was like, "no, we're going to break with that". I think it looks like a wedding monogram. I see the fish too though.

In terms of what young people want to see right now... I don't know. I'm literally being hired to do so much consulting around this question, but what's funny is that I can only speak for myself, really. But I did have a conversation with this other curator yesterday in London, and we were speaking about how an artist is not an artist any more. Fashion is not just fashion any more. Everything is very intertwined. I don't even know if I identify just as an editor. Maybe I'm like an editor-curator hybrid. Maybe I don't have a title. Also, this goes for the way we approach art now, it's not just traditional visual art. Fashion can be visual art, music is a part of visual art. I think it's very fluid. We know how to pull things from different media and it's very exciting.

SB

What you're saying is interesting. Does it really happen like that, some company contacts you to explain what young people want?

EBO

All the time. They're trying to wrap their head around this new generation. Like, "how can we reach a young person?" I mean, the only thing I say to them: you can all hear my secret. And it's very simple: involve young people themselves in order to get a young audience. That's the way to go. Young people don't listen to their parents, they listen to their friends. It's peer-to-peer. You can't be a 50-year-old tied-up CEO and decide "Now I'm going to sell something this way to a young person".

SB

Other questions?

AM

In this fluid context that you're talking about, do you ever imagine yourself going into a classroom after all your experience being an editor and learning on the ground? Do you imagine studying something or do you even imagine becoming a teacher instead of a student?

EBO

Well, I was saying that if I'm going to go back to school, I'm going to be a doctor. I'm going to do something completely different or completely academic. Everybody says "don't quit school" and I guess, "yeah, don't quit school", but I don't know.

I felt that there was so much more out there for me, and I was really impatient and school was going to take a long time. It was just not the right time. I think school is really fun, I had a great time, but it was just the fact that you have to be there from Monday to Friday, 9 to 5. Now there can be a whole new way of going to school. You can study on Skype now, you can have classes online. I think this is going to be redefined in the next few years. I don't know if I want to be a teacher though, but to come and have these lectures and meet all of you guys and students and I think that is very admirable. It takes a lot of discipline to be a student. I can't be like "do this, do that", but I can have open conversations and share my story.

AM

With your own vision and experience, can you give young people who have the dream of starting a new project any advice or feedback?

EBO

I think there's a lot to be said, but I don't know if I can be so specific as these are all individual experiences. There are a lot of brands out there and they have the money and there's a lot of money in the system. I guess my advice would be to simply take the money from them. It's a circle: the money is going to be in the circle anyway. So you might as well take some and use it for what you feel is for the better. I said this in my documentary. I think we have to be a little bit ruthless because there is money out there and we need money to realize our ideas. Go and grab it.

SB

If the money is out there, someone is going to take it.
Be the first one.

EBO
And use the internet. Reach out, use the internet for what it's worth. Promote yourself. Create your own network.

AM
Thank you, because I didn't know you at all and I'm here and I'm really happy to listen to this conversation. So thank you first of all. Young people typically don't have a lot of money. I can't really go to museums, even if I want to, because I have 50 euros a month and it's not even mine. Magazines are expensive, a luxury. So if I want to buy yours, I might not be able to afford it.

EBO
Come up to me and I'll give you a copy. In general, I think this is always tricky when you're trying to create a product. I'm not selling Wallet because I'm making any profit from it. But I have a team, there are expenses. So it's always a way to justify that. I was seriously thinking about making Wallet free at some point and that would have been great. Then I realized that there's going to be nobody distributing the magazine for you, because the distribution houses are dependent on making their percentage. And if you're going to distribute it yourself, online, there are expenses with that too. So it's tricky. I agree and I feel the same. But meanwhile, Wallet is in the cheapest price range; there are magazines that are 40 euros and even more.

SB
There's a big effort to make it economical. Wallet comes out every three months, right?

EBO
Every third month, or three times a year. I'm not so strict about it though. I don't want to have a really strict publishing schedule,

but we have to work with brands, and they need to know when it's going to come out.

AM

Most of my friends and I are sad because we cannot buy magazines. We have to go to the public library.

EBO

Libraries are fantastic though. I think the library is an extremely important resource that should not be underestimated. But you can also get five friends together and buy a Wallet. That's two euros each. I'm going to give you copies though!

AM

I just wanted to say thank you for talking. I teach editorial design here and I'm a magazine freak. I've read Recens Paper since issue three and I loved it initially because of the way you treated the advertisements. I thought it was so funny! Apropos libraries, I want to say to all the students who can't get access to magazines: go upstairs, ask the library to get a subscription, you will make everybody happy and the editorial design department will become better in the future. And I wanted to ask you Elise something if it's not too indiscreet: how many issues do you print every circulation?

EBO

About 3000. It varies around each issue's economy. If we can afford it, we print 3000, but between 2000 or 3000.

AM

Thank you. It's a bright spark on the horizon.

EBO

Great. Thank you for having me!

AM
Welcome back to Barcelona, I want to thank you for coming. What you say here is really inspirational. You said you didn't have a studio. I would like to know what your life is like, what your day-to-day is like, where you are living, what you do. Not everything, just a snapshot.

EBO
Well, I'm from Oslo, Norway. I guess I'm based there at the moment, but I travel a lot. I've been very lucky to get all of these opportunities to see the world at a very young age. I know, it's a real cliché, but it's been so helpful. Every day is very different, as I do a lot of different things. I'm working on a series of books, curating exhibitions, developing a new institution, doing talks and consulting… As well as working on Wallet, which is a little bit of a side project now. Wallet doesn't take up as much time as for example Recens used to do, because it's only 60 pages, it's three conversations and the visual essay. I guess what I spend the most time doing is having conversations with people online, on calls or in meetings. And lots of emails, stuff like that, administrative things. I'm the employer and the employee so I can basically choose when I wake up in the morning, or if I want to work at all that day. In that sense, my income, my results, everything depends on me. I can't really say there's an everyday routine or regime, and there's a lot of freedom in that.

AM
You were saying earlier, when you were 13, 14 years old, you had a Facebook group and you were working in this online forum. How has this part influenced your work? Do you still work online? What is the percentage?

EBO
As long as I have WiFi, I can work from anywhere. I don't work through Facebook chats anymore, but I'd say a good 75% of my work happens on my phone or my computer. At least.

AM
Thank you.

AM
I wanted to ask you if you ever have any doubts about what you do, because you seem very brave and you stick with the idea of what you do.

EBO
Thank you! I think this is partly why it's been really great to have projects over a specific amount of time, more temporary projects. Recens was only seven issues and I had the freedom to step away after that. Wallet is also very flexible. But of course, I do doubt. I'm growing up and trying to figure out how to sustain a living and all those things. I also think I have a very clear narrative in the back of my mind and a strong intuition. My past two, four, six years have been impossible to foresee. So I'm trying not to predict anything, but I am strategic and I have a narrative, a direction I want to go in for now, but always open to leaving that and doing something else also.

SB
Any other questions?

AM
You said school's fine, but do you think that in design or in any arts, having a creative degree is actually useful or would you say that it's just unnecessary?

EBO
That completely depends on what you make out of it yourself. Of course, if you have a degree it weighs heavy if you want to apply for a job. But if you work for yourself, I don't think it necessarily matters principally. I do think there's a lot of really amazing things that can happen from having an education and having that time and space for reflection and discipline. I think the previous generations had a whole different expectation of leaving university and getting a job, that kind of journey. For us, it's more about leaving university and navigating your way through everything. I think the future of working, especially in the creative fields, is definitely freelance. There's a lot of insourcing talent on a project basis. I think it's rare nowadays that people are actually employed permanently in a space.

SB
I think that as we've been saying, it's not about having a degree or a BA. It's about what it means to study something. But you, Elise, you've been studying for many years in a way. Maybe there's not a paper that says you've been doing it, but the important thing is the content and how you use that content to produce something or to start something...

EBO
...even just to have a reflection in your own mind.
Sometimes people need to be pushed to do that too,
to be confronted with themselves. I think it's important.

AM
I would like to ask you what your journey is going to be for the following years? What do you expect, what do you think the future is going to be like?

EBO
That's a very big question. Again, I would have never guessed two years ago that I would be where I am today, and that I'm in touch with the people that I am, and getting the offers that I do. I'm also not a big fan of talking about my upcoming projects, I like to work on them in silence and let the result be the noise. But lately I've been thinking a lot about digital loss and physical preservation. What's going to happen with all the material that's out there, and all these Instagram feeds or Facebook memories, in, let's say, 10 years? Like we touched upon earlier, there's an increasing priority for digitization, but not for archiving and preservation of physical material. I think it's completely crucial to guard, document and archive all this material now. So I'm working with that idea, consolidated in one space. In addition to many new exciting projects in the realm of media, fashion, publishing, curating and criticism... We'll see in two years. Let's stay in touch!

SB
We'll let two years go by and we'll see what happens.

EBO
I'll be back!

SB
Great, let's round up then. Thank you all so much for being here Elise!

EBO
I'm going to stick around, so just come and say hi and get a copy of Wallet. Thanks again for having me!

AM
[Applause]

In publishing, as in music, youth meant business.

Generation-defining music is often done by young people for young people. It is a language, often coded, that draws people in and brings them together; congregating peers and people in the knowing. Much as did zines, pamphlets and indie magazines, each with its own messages, only heard by the community gathered around the same skate park, club or band. The mythology of the teen band and that of the disruptive new magazine runs parallel. In what is possibly the last great era of culture-shaping publications, the alchemy between music and publishing gave us The Face and New Wave in the 1980s, and Dazed & Confused and the London club scene in the 1990s.

Then came the internet. In a short space of time, digital culture changed this paradigm forever. The internet killed the magazine star. Social media, from Friendster to TikTok, via MySpace, Facebook and Instagram, has reshaped the way young people communicate with each other. It has made it instant, borderless and free. Flickr, and then Tumblr built an international community around visual ideas, codes, aesthetics. Image-makers gathered around these platforms as they once had around magazines. Technology has offered a means to distribute ideas without the limitation imposed by the production and distribution of a physical object. You just need a computer (now a phone) and an internet connection.

So how does Elise By Olsen's publishing practice – through Recens Paper and later Wallet – fit into this narrative? It subverts it. I like to think that even as a 13-year-old, wanting to publish her magazine – designed in a Word document, printed in 1000 copies and with a strong distribution ambition – By Olsen wasn't ever nostalgic – "dreaming of the golden age of Sleazenation" – but subversive. Maybe even subconsciously so. Recens Paper might not have been subversive in its content, but the act of publishing it was.

Not to stretch the analogy between publishing and music too far, but I cannot help thinking about how live gigs have counterbalanced the digitalization of music with a physical and community experience. Yes, it is great to have Spotify access to all the music in the world, but gathering together with musicians in a shared space is a different thing. Similarly magazines, an objectively obsolete mode of communication in our increasingly digital culture, which offer a physical experience, ranging from the act of purchasing to the act of reading and collecting. Magazines demand space; they become part of our physical existence, and in doing so they overtly represent us.

Making or publishing a magazine can be a form of subversion, and so can buying them. It is a way of asserting who you are in opposition to others and to do so in a specific fashion, by picking up a publication that represents you and your set of beliefs. Today 'the magazine' has become an identity index, rather than merely a holder of information. Fashion – further away from its utilitarian primary function – is also an identity index: with a piece of clothing we awarely or unawarely project onto others a coded message of who we are – or believe we are, or want to be. So it is not surprising that the union between fashion and magazines is the one that still survives: they both function similarly.

In a world that has finally woken up to the climate emergency, where the digital is replacing the real-world version in ever more aspects of our life, it's hard to know if Elise By Olsen is fighting a belligerent rearguard action against the inevitable or is one of the first digital natives to have redefined the function of magazines in our times. Or perhaps it's both. As a former teenager who collected hundreds of publications which are still stored in my parents' house, I say: magazines are dead, long live magazines.